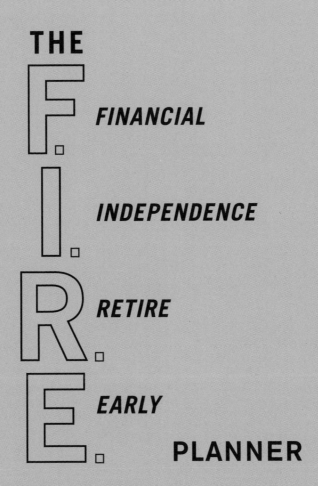

THE

# F. FINANCIAL

# I. INDEPENDENCE

# R. RETIRE

# E. EARLY

PLANNER

# DEDICATIONS

To my mom, who gave me the love of reading and inspiration to write a book

To my dad, who taught me the power of frugality, cash flow, and focus

To my rich uncles, who gave me the gift of possibility

To my wife, who made my life so rich long before financial independence

And to my kids, who will lead the next generation through love, courage, and kindness

# THE

## F.I.R.E.

MICHAEL QUAN
*of the personal-finance blog*
**Financially Alert**

**FINANCIAL**

**INDEPENDENCE**

**RETIRE**

A STEP-BY-STEP
WORKBOOK TO
REACH YOUR
FULL FINANCIAL
POTENTIAL

**EARLY**

# PLANNER

TILLER PRESS

New York   London   Toronto   Sydney   New Delhi

TILLER PRESS

An Imprint of Simon & Schuster, Inc.
1230 Avenue of the Americas
New York, NY 10020

First Tiller Press paperback edition May 2021

TILLER PRESS and colophon are trademarks of Simon & Schuster, Inc.

For information about special discounts for bulk purchases, please contact Simon & Schuster Special Sales at 1-866-506-1949 or business@simonandschuster.com.

The Simon & Schuster Speakers Bureau can bring authors to your live event. For more information or to book an event, contact the Simon & Schuster Speakers Bureau at 1-866-248-3049 or visit our website at www.simonspeakers.com.

Senior Commissioning Editor: Eszter Karpati
Editor: Rachel Malig
Art Director: Gemma Wilson
Designer: Nikki Ellis
Design concept: Eoghan O'Brien
Publisher: Samantha Warrington

Manufactured in China

10  9  8  7  6  5  4  3  2  1

Library of Congress Cataloging-in-Publication Data has been applied for.

ISBN 978-1-9821-6965-7
ISBN 978-1-9821-7876-5 (ebook)

# CONTENTS

Meet Michael  6

How to Use This Planner as Your Guide  8

## CHAPTER 1
**Introduction to FIRE  11**

    What is FIRE?  12

    Why you should pursue FIRE  18

    Who can achieve FIRE?  22

    When is the best time to start?  27

## CHAPTER 2
**The FIRE Mindset  33**

    Money beliefs  34

    Aligning actions  44

## CHAPTER 3
**Your FIRE Numbers  47**

    The importance of knowing
      your numbers  48

    Debt  52

    Cash flow  56

    Net worth  60

    Using technology to save time  62

    How to track your FIRE numbers
      with technology  64

    The FIRE equation  66

    Defining financial
      independence  68

## CHAPTER 4
**Ways to Achieve FIRE  73**

    Focusing on FI  74

    Compound interest  76

    Developing new habits  78

    Saving for FIRE  80

    Investing for FIRE  96

    Real estate investing for FIRE  108

    Entrepreneurship for FIRE  120

## CHAPTER 5
**Designing Your FIRE Plan 135**

    Getting started  136

    Start with the end in mind  138

    Outline your FIRE strategy  150

    Map your FIRE milestones &
      celebration points  152

    Taking massive action  155

    Evaluating, adjusting &
      achieving results  158

    Achieve the desired outcome  160

## CHAPTER 6
**You're on FIRE—Now What?  165**

    Celebrate!  166

    Retiring early  168

    Post FIRE  177

Acknowledgments  188

Glossary  189

Notes  190

Index  191

# Meet *Michael*

**HI, MY NAME IS MICHAEL QUAN, AND WELCOME TO**
*THE FIRE PLANNER.*

Ever since I was young, I've been fascinated by money. I had the rare opportunity to observe two uncles who had done very well for themselves financially and always found it curious that they didn't need to go to work like my own parents or those of my friends. Instead, these uncles got to take their kids to and from school, pursue hobbies and business ventures, and vacation anytime they wished. I remember thinking, "Wow. I want that when I get older!" I didn't know it at the time, but they had achieved FI (financial independence), and their money was now working hard for them.

This knowledge that FI was even possible has been my unfair advantage. I reasoned that if my uncles could achieve FI, then why couldn't I? And that's exactly what I set out to do. I read over a hundred personal finance and personal development books, attended dozens of seminars, and spent tens of thousands of dollars educating myself on the best strategies I could use to get ahead.

In 2001, when I was twenty-five years old, I cofounded an IT support company with some friends. We had humble beginnings, but managed to build a very profitable service company over ten years. We expanded nationally and then sold the company to a larger service provider. This allowed me to cash out some business equity, and I then put that money back to work in real estate investments.

After selling the company, I spent another eighteen months working for the new owners, and during this process I realized quickly that a nine-to-five corporate job was not for me. After I ran some quick numbers with my wife, we realized that we had accumulated a sizable base of assets. We had been saving and investing aggressively over the past few years and were now FI (financially independent), or very close to it. Once this became apparent, I negotiated a severance package and dove headfirst into early retirement at age thirty-six.

Achieving FIRE (financial independence, retire early) has lived up to all my dreams and more. I get to be fully present with my young family on a daily basis and have the complete freedom to pursue passion projects, businesses, and even international fishing trips.

I tell you this not to impress you but to impress upon you that achieving FIRE is possible. If I can do it, then you can too. Trust me.

Remember that unfair advantage I had? Well, I'm passing that along to you now. The only difference is that this book will cover everything you need to know: *The FIRE Planner* outlines the exact steps to achieve FIRE. It's the book I wish I'd had from the beginning.

Enjoy the journey, friend!

# "LIFE MOVES PRETTY FAST. IF YOU DON'T STOP TO LOOK AROUND ONCE IN A WHILE, YOU COULD MISS IT."

**FERRIS BUELLER**
*Ferris Bueller's Day Off*

# HOW TO USE THIS PLANNER
## *as your guide*

## WELCOME TO THE FIRE PLANNER

**THIS INTERACTIVE PLANNER HAS BEEN DESIGNED TO EDUCATE AND GUIDE YOU EVERY STEP OF THE WAY ALONG YOUR PERSONAL JOURNEY TO FIRE (FINANCIAL INDEPENDENCE, RETIRE EARLY).**

### The planner is laid out in six sections:

**CHAPTER 1:** Introduction to FIRE
**CHAPTER 2:** The FIRE Mindset
**CHAPTER 3:** Your FIRE Numbers
**CHAPTER 4:** Ways to Achieve FIRE
**CHAPTER 5:** Designing your FIRE Plan
**CHAPTER 6:** You're on FIRE—
　　　　　　　Now What?

There should be something of value here for students at every stage of their FIRE journey.

If you're a beginner, welcome to the wonderful world of FIRE! I invite you to take your time and explore with an open mind. The concepts are explained as simply as possible, although there may be some jargon that will seem unfamiliar. If you find yourself confused, fantastic! That means you're learning. There's also a full glossary on page 189 in case you need a reference.

For those of you who have already started your journey to FIRE, this planner will give you some additional structure to work within. Perhaps you've missed a step or are looking for options. All you need is one good

idea to change everything. Also, take the time to explore the mindset of this journey (see The Fire Mindset, pages 33–45)—it's an easy part to miss if you begin the journey alone.

*With that said, many of the topics I cover are much more nuanced than I'm able to go into here. There are so many fascinating tangents to explore on your path to FIRE, so I encourage you to deepen your understanding of those particular strategies or concepts by taking the time to educate yourself further.*

### Throughout the planner you will find interactive elements:

- Worksheets/Journals
- Case Studies
- FIRE Tips
- Did You Knows

Learning is not a passive activity. While reading is a wonderful start, putting pen to paper helps to lock in intentions. And that's why *The FIRE Planner* is designed to be interactive: I want you to be an active participant so you can have the best chance of achieving FI.

I encourage you to take the time to write in this planner. In fact, let's start now. Go ahead and tell me your name and the date on which you're filling in this section.

_____

_____

_____

Write about what compelled you to pick up this book. Are you tired of living the same routine? Or are you perhaps inspired by possibility?

_____

_____

_____

_____

_____

_____

_____

_____

_____

_____

_____

_____

_____

_____

_____

_____

_____

_____

_____

_____

_____

_____

_____

_____

_____

Finally, while you can do this on your own, it's more fun to share the journey with others! Consider finding an accountability partner and going through *The FIRE Planner* together. You can bounce ideas off each other and get a different perspective.

Happy FIRE planning!

What is **FIRE**?

Why you should pursue **FIRE**

Who can achieve **FIRE**?

When is the best time to **START**?

# 1

## Introduction

### TO

# FIRE

# *What is* **FIRE?**

THE BASIC CONCEPT OF FIRE IS TO FOCUS YOUR EFFORTS ON SAVING AND INVESTING (UP TO 70%), COMMIT TO LIVING A SIMPLER LIFESTYLE, AND CUT YOUR RETIREMENT DATE BY DECADES.

**F** inancial

**I** ndependence

**R** etire

**E** arly

What a catchy acronym! Who wouldn't want to have financial independence and be able to retire early?

If you've picked up this book, then no doubt this idea appeals to you too. In this section, we'll discover the basic components of FIRE and discuss why you could, and should, pursue FIRE.

With diligence and compounding interest on your side, your efforts will be rewarded with a nest egg large enough to (slowly) withdraw from . . . indefinitely.

TO START, LET'S COVER SOME TERMS YOU'LL WANT TO BE FAMILIAR WITH

**FI (Financial Independence)** = when passive income equals or exceeds your living expenses and you're no longer reliant on earned income or dependent on others

**RE (Retire Early)** = retiring at a much earlier age than traditional standards (e.g., age thirty instead of age sixty-five), which enables you to pursue your interests without requiring additional income

**Income** = money that comes into your household from a job, investments, or other means

**Active or Earned Income** = money received from active work (e.g., a job, a business you operate, etc.)

**Passive Income** = money received that doesn't require you to actively work (e.g., dividends, royalties, rental income, certain types of business income, etc.)

FI IS ARGUABLY THE MOST IMPORTANT PART OF FIRE BECAUSE IT'S USED TO DESCRIBE A POINT IN TIME WHEN YOUR PASSIVE INCOME EQUALS OR EXCEEDS YOUR MONTHLY EXPENSES. TO BETTER UNDERSTAND THIS, LET'S LOOK AT A FEW EXAMPLES.

## Example 1

Paul has a job that earns him $60,000, or $5,000 per month. He has monthly expenses of $3,500 (taxes, rent, food, insurance, transportation, etc.).

**Is he financially independent?**
No. Paul is not financially independent. Even though he has a surplus of cash each month, he still needs to work for income.

## Example 2

Jennifer has a job that earns her $50,000, or $4,167 per month. She also owns five rental properties that provide her with $2,500 of passive income per month. Her monthly expenses are $4,500.

**Is she financially independent?**
No. Although Jennifer is well on her way to achieving financial independence, she still has a shortfall of $2,000 per month *not* covered by passive income.

## Example 3

Dave has a part-time job that earns him $36,000, or $3,000 per month. He also owns ten rental properties that provide him with $5,000 of passive income per month. His monthly expenses are $4,000.

**Is Dave financially independent?**
Yes. Dave's rental properties bring in enough passive income every month to exceed his expenses of $4,000. Thus, Dave technically does not need to work his part-time job in order to meet his monthly expenses.

Next, let's discuss RE, or "retire early." Once you hit FI you have freedom of choice! Since your monthly expenses are fully covered by your passive income, you no longer have to actively work for earned income. You are free to "retire early."

At this point, you could sit on the beach all day long and your expenses would still be taken care of. Or you could volunteer, start a business, write a book . . . the options are endless, and the choice is yours!

# THE MODERN FIRE MOVEMENT

**FI EXISTED LONG BEFORE FIRE BECAME A POPULAR CONCEPT IN TODAY'S CULTURE. HOWEVER, THE MODERN FIRE MOVEMENT IS UNIQUE IN THAT IDEAS CAN BE SPREAD QUICKER THAN EVER.**

With the rise of the Internet, websites evolved from static pages sharing basic information to full-blown dynamic and interactive sites. Now we enjoy blogs with daily updates, rich media-like photos and video, and even applications that can do complex calculations (e.g., Monte Carlo simulations). Soon we will be living in a world where AR (augmented reality) and VR (virtual reality) are just a part of daily life.

## Where did the modern FIRE movement come from?

We all love a good story. And when sites like Early Retirement Extreme (earlyretirementextreme.com) and Mr. Money Mustache (mrmoneymustache .com) championed and modeled the idea that retirement could occur decades earlier than usual, people were fascinated.

The premise was simple. By focusing on extreme savings and investing, you could feasibly cut the retirement age in half. And ideas such as intentional spending and living a simple life resonated with millions of people around the world.

**People are waking up and beginning to question the traditional advice of:**

Go to school, get good grades

Go to college, get good grades

Get a job, work your way up

Retire when you're sixty-five

I am a proponent of higher education, yet going to university doesn't guarantee you a career, or even a job, for that matter. You need more than good grades and a degree to be successful these days.

In today's job markets, you'll find a dynamic marketplace that no longer rewards you for staying at a single company until retirement. Instead, the new generations know it's reasonable to change jobs, and even careers, multiple times in one's life.

**WORK FOR MONEY**

**MAKE MONEY WORK FOR YOU**

## Common characteristics of those on the path to FIRE:

✓ Save/invest aggressively (30% to 70% of earned income)

✓ Invest in broad, low-cost index funds (e.g., VTSAX—Vanguard's Total Stock Market Index Fund)

✓ Seek to live a simpler life; reduce or eliminate wasteful spending

✓ Focus on experiences over things

✓ Use the 4% Rule to determine your FI baseline (see page 66)

Workers from older generations are being replaced with cheaper labor and technology, so it's now a requirement to keep creating value and reinventing yourself throughout your entire career.

Even those who've followed a traditional path are coming up empty-handed; it's all too common to see stories of retirees forced to go back to work because their finances weren't in order, or because they were simply unprepared.

Most important, if you're required to work until age sixty-five, then aren't you giving away the prime years of your life to somebody else?

So it's apparent that the traditional model may no longer be relevant.

The modern FIRE movement offers something far more exciting and practical. It offers choice, and the promise of financial freedom to those who are bold enough to reach for it.

But you must be willing to take the time to plan, understand what you value, and learn to make your money work for you—and you're in the right place to start!

FIRE falls into the realm of personal finance. So let's remember that FIRE should therefore reflect your personal goals, values, and aspirations. That means your FIRE goals may not match mine.

As you'll see, there are many different ways to achieve FIRE, and I encourage you to explore the full spectrum of strategies available. For now, though, it's good to learn what a baseline looks like within the modern FIRE movement.

# VARIATIONS OF FIRE

**ONE OF THE BEST THINGS ABOUT FIRE IS THAT YOU CAN DO IT YOUR WAY. THERE'S NO ONE PERFECT FORMULA THAT FITS ALL.**

In fact, there are many different ways to express FIRE, and some catchy names to go with them. As we explore these, ask yourself which one appeals to you most.

Remember, FIRE is the point at which your passive income equals or exceeds your expenses and you're able to retire early. So let's take a peek at the most basic FIRE formula. We'll cover this in greater depth later, but for now remember this:

**25 x Your Annual Expenses = Your FIRE Number** (i.e., your nest egg)

So if your annual expenses are $40,000, then 25 x $40,000 = $1,000,000

Next, we'll use a generally accepted annual withdrawal rate of 4% from your $1,000,000 portfolio. In most scenarios, this should last you thirty years or more.

Simple, right? Now let's check out the different types of FIRE. Bear in mind that there are no standard definitions of FIRE quite yet, so you may see a variety of definitions of the same terms online.

*First, we want to note that the average American household spends about $60,000 per year.*

**LeanFIRE**: Targeted annual spending is half of $60,000, so $30,000 x 25 = $750,000

**RegularFIRE** (or FIRE): Target of $60,000 x 25 = $1,500,000

**FatFIRE**: Target of $100,000+ x 25 = $2,500,000+

**BaristaFIRE**: Has achieved FI and chooses to work part-time for supplemental income and/or access to benefits; a variation is if one spouse is retired and the other continues to work (by choice, not necessity)

## Goal Amount to be Financially Independent
Most people expect to be FI with **$1,000,000** or less

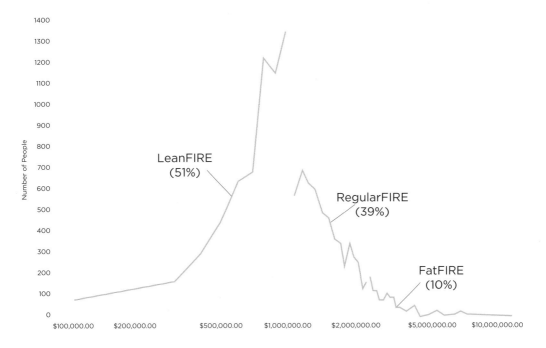

As you may imagine, your ability to reach some or all of these levels will depend on two key factors: your income and your expenses.

During the course of the book we'll spend a fair amount of time exploring different ways to optimize each of these variables in your life, and I think you'll be happily surprised to see just how much control you actually have over them.

### Did you know?

When more than one thousand aspiring FIRE seekers were surveyed, we learned that **51%** of participants were seeking LeanFIRE; **39%** were seeking RegularFIRE; and only **10%** were seeking FatFIRE.

# *Why you should pursue* FIRE

**DO YOU EVER GET A NAGGING FEELING THAT THERE'S MORE TO DO IN YOUR LIFE? HAVE YOU EVER DREAMED ABOUT WHAT YOU WOULD DO IF YOU WON THE LOTTERY? HAVE YOU QUESTIONED YOUR CAREER PATH?**

If so, you're in good company.

Reaching for FIRE is a courageous pursuit. As we have learned, the conventional metrics for success are defined by money, cash flow, and lifestyle.

Yet the journey to FIRE is so much more. It's an odyssey of self-exploration and growth. It's a path to free yourself of limitations and to positively impact those around you in a truly remarkable way.

The journey to FIRE is anything but easy, but the freedom you'll achieve is well worth the effort required.

Pursuing FIRE can help you to live your best life, and I believe that your best life appears when you're chasing your true potential.

All too often we limit ourselves with the internal chatter swirling inside our heads: "I'm not good enough"; "That's not who I am"; "That will never work"; "I'm too lazy"; "I'm too old"; "I'm too young." These self-doubts and limiting beliefs paralyze us and keep us from moving forward.

But the truth is that you are special. You weren't designed to swim in the shallow end of life. On the contrary: you're here to do extraordinary things.

The fact is that you didn't ask for this life, and yet it was given to you. You're a biological lottery winner who beat the odds billions of times over: you're blessed with a heart that beats life into you over one hundred thousand times every day without your ever asking, and you're gifted with specific abilities and talents that are unique only to you. That's the truth.

When you come to the end of your life, how will you define success? Will your life be full of beautiful memories, treasured relationships, and a legacy of impact? Or will it be full of regret and sadness, knowing that you had more to give?

Embarking on the path to FIRE is your opportunity to break out of the rat race. No longer do you need to be told how to do something simply to take home a paycheck. Instead, you're declaring your independence from the bondage of old paradigms and reclaiming your right to pursue life beyond money.

The choice is yours.

*What* **IS YOUR** **WHY?**

# FINDING YOUR WHY WORKSHEET

There's no question that I'm passionate about FIRE and that I want you to be too. However, what I want for you is not nearly as important as what you want for yourself. You must take full ownership of your decision to pursue FIRE because the journey is a marathon, not a sprint.

In this section, I'd like you to develop a compelling *why* for yourself. Why should you pursue FIRE? What will it mean to you? Your *why* should be deeply rooted in your values so there's never any hesitation in knowing what the right answer is.

Finally, your *why* should give you a clear sense of purpose and bring you fulfillment as you strive toward your FIRE goal.

Here are a few examples to get you thinking. The clearer you can be about your goals, the better.

- To be a fully present parent
- To travel the world with my spouse
- To start the business I've always wanted
- To meet my full potential
- To make an impact in this world
- To build meaningful relationships
- To make daily work into play
- To master the game of money
- To be a leader by example

**What's your *why* for reaching FIRE? List the individual reasons below:**

1. _____
2. _____
3. _____
4. _____

**What does your best life look like? Who will you share it with?**

_____
_____
_____
_____
_____
_____
_____

**Are you capable of achieving FIRE? Why?**

_____
_____
_____
_____
_____
_____
_____

# PERSONAL GROWTH

**THE HAPPY SIDE EFFECT OF DECIDING TO PURSUE FIRE IS AN OPTIONAL PARALLEL JOURNEY OF PERSONAL GROWTH.**

Seeking FIRE and personal growth go together like tea and honey. Sure, you could reach FIRE without the personal-growth journey, but why not take it if the ride will be that much sweeter?

## Personal growth

Also known as personal development, this covers activities that improve awareness and identity, develop talents and potential, build human capital and facilitate employability, enhance quality of life, and contribute to the realization of dreams and aspirations.

Personal growth doesn't stop with your mind—it should also carry over to your physical well-being. Your body's health and energy levels have a direct effect on your emotions and thoughts, so by learning to manage your physical states, your journey will be much more enjoyable. And who would want to FIRE if they're sick all the time?

By simultaneously focusing on your personal growth, you're much more likely to achieve balance on your journey to FIRE. Just because you're able to save 90% of your income doesn't necessarily mean that you should. Finding balance means you become good at evaluating opportunity costs and comparing them against your values. If you know your personal values well, you'll avoid getting sucked into serving money for money's sake.

Never forget that money is just the tool that will allow you to reach the freedom you desire. As you accumulate more money, it will simply become a magnification of who you are, so it's best to be happy with who you are once you've gotten all the money you need.

Growth in life or FIRE is not a constant ascent—rather, it is filled with peaks and valleys along the way. The only real constant in this journey is change, and obstacles are inevitable. Maybe the markets turn the wrong way, or maybe you get hit with an unexpected expense that turns your world upside down. Persistence and determination will see you through to the other side, fueled by your *why*.

You cannot plan for everything that happens to you in life, but you can *always* control your perspective.

> ## "TO CHANGE OURSELVES EFFECTIVELY, WE FIRST HAD TO CHANGE OUR PERCEPTIONS."
> **Stephen R. Covey**

# CONTRIBUTION & GIVING BACK

**AS A FINANCIAL COACH WHO SPECIALIZES IN HELPING PEOPLE ACHIEVE FINANCIAL FREEDOM, I'VE NOTICED AN INTERESTING COMMON CHARACTERISTIC AMONG THOSE SEEKING FI. EVERYONE, AT SOME LEVEL, IS LOOKING TO CONTRIBUTE VALUE TO THIS WORLD, AND FOR A WAY TO GIVE BACK. CHANCES ARE GOOD THAT YOU'RE SOMEONE WHO CARES ABOUT THIS AS WELL.**

Once your basic needs are met, money is simply a tool and a metric to grow. By finding abundance along your path to FIRE, you will provide hope to others, and you will naturally be inclined to give more.

Contribution and giving back are the ultimate paths to fulfillment. However, don't wait until you reach FIRE to be generous—the time to start is now. By giving first, you open yourself up to being able to receive more. This is true in a psychological sense as well as a spiritual one.

Giving can take many forms, and there's always something you can give each day. If you can't give money, give your time; if you can't give your time, give your wisdom and intentions. Giving can also mean leading by example. The possibilities are endless.

When all is said and done, you cannot take your money with you when you're gone. So you're simply a steward of "your money" for a sliver of time. What will you do with it? Who will you be remembered as? We'll dive deeper into this in the post-FIRE section.

For now, answer these two questions:

**How will your journey to FIRE allow you to contribute in new ways?**

**What would you give to this world if money were no object?**

# Who can achieve FIRE?

**AT FIRST GLANCE, FIRE MAY SEEM LIKE A NOVELTY FOR HIGH-INCOME EARNERS ONLY. BUT WOULD YOU BE SURPRISED TO LEARN THAT ORDINARY PEOPLE ARE ALSO ACHIEVING FIRE?**

Yes, it's true. Achieving FIRE is relative. This means that financial independence is based on your own lifestyle, not someone else's. So if you can be happy spending only $30,000 per year, the number for you to achieve FIRE is going to be much less than someone who requires $90,000 per year. We'll discuss in later sections how to calculate this for yourself, as it will become the baseline for your FIRE number.

Let's look at some of the common "Income" categories of FIRE seekers. It's quite possible that you'll find yourself fitting into more than one of these over the course of your FIRE journey.

**SINKS—Single Income No Kids:**
These individuals are typically younger professionals just getting started with their careers; they have yet to settle down and only need to provide for themselves at this point. This is a great time to get a jump start on FIRE, although sometimes at this age, partying can seem more worthwhile.

**SIKS—Single Income Kids:**
These individuals are typically divorced or widowed parents; they have a single income and need to provide for themselves and one or more children. This category is at a disadvantage for achieving FIRE, although it's not impossible.

**DINKS—Dual Income No Kids:**
These couples are typically married and have two strong incomes; because they're both working and have no children to support, this category is often considered the most advantaged for building a FIRE nest egg. If both partners make a strong enough income, then it's relatively simple for them to set aside one of their incomes to save and invest, placing them in a strong position to achieve FIRE.

**DIKS—Dual Income Kids:**
These couples are both working and decided to have one or more children; because they need to support kids, their incomes are partially directed toward raising them. If they have two strong incomes and live below their means, they still have an excellent chance of reaching FIRE.

# CASE STUDY
## FIRE Celebrity Pete Adeney (MMM)

Pete Adeney, better known as Mr. Money Mustache (MMM), retired early at just thirty years old. A former software engineer, Pete decided to save the majority of his income and invest the proceeds in stock market index funds.

He started his blog—mrmoneymustache.com—back in 2011, and it became wildly popular. Pete is adamant about lowering your consumer-minded wastefulness (by 50% or more) and getting back to living instead. He and his family own one car and use it only when hauling large items. Otherwise, you'll find him happily riding his bike whenever he needs to go somewhere.

I believe Pete's genius has really been in identifying hedonic adaptation as a primary reason to break the cycle of spending. Hedonic adaptation is the tendency for you to revert back to similar levels of happiness regardless of major shifts in life, positive or negative. Because of this tendency, Pete basically tells us that purchasing "things" will not make us inherently more happy in the long run.

It's true, right? Think about a purchase that you *really* wanted for a long time. So long that the anticipation was killing you! And, when you finally got it, you had a burst of happiness. Unfortunately, that feeling fades quickly, and you revert back to your normal level of happiness, even though you still have this new purchase in your possession.

So, Mr. MM asks, why are you chasing external things? Why not chase freedom instead and break the hedonic adaptation consumer cycle?

Pete likes to say he's accidentally started a cult; he calls his most loyal followers "Mustachians." This has spawned many online groups across the globe who share his ideas, and Pete has been featured in numerous media outlets, including CNBC, MarketWatch, the *Washington Post*, and the *New Yorker*.

A final point of admiration for Pete is around the integrity of his ideas. He's inadvertently earned many thousands of dollars from his blog over the years, but that hasn't stopped him from living according to the principles he teaches.

> ## "GETTING RICH IS MORE MENTAL THAN IT IS TACTICAL."
>
> **Pete Adeney (MMM)**

# CASE STUDY
## FI/FIRE Profiles

AS A PERSONAL FINANCE BLOGGER, I'VE HAD THE PRIVILEGE OF
LEARNING ABOUT OTHER PEOPLE'S PATHS TO FIRE. THOSE WHO'VE
ACHIEVED FI/FIRE COME FROM DIFFERENT BACKGROUNDS AND
LOCATIONS. THIS IS A SMALL SAMPLING OF PUBLIC BLOGGERS YOU
MAY FIND ONLINE. HOWEVER, THERE ARE COUNTLESS PRIVATE
CITIZENS AROUND THE GLOBE WHO ENJOY A FIRE LIFESTYLE TOO;
YOU NEVER KNOW WHO YOU'RE SITTING NEXT TO!

**Name:** Dustin Heiner
(Successfully Unemployed)
**Former Work:** Government Employee
**FI/FIRE Age:** Thirty-Seven
**Source/FI Accelerator:** Real Estate
Investments

**Name:** Leif Dahleen
(Physician on FIRE)
**Former Work:** Physician
**FI/FIRE Age:** Forty-Three
**Source/FI Accelerator:** Stock
Investments

**Name:** Annie
(Goodegg Investments)
**Former Work:** Teacher
**FI/FIRE Age:** Thirties
**Source/FI Accelerator:** Stock
Investments

**Name:** Kim (Frugal Engineers)
**Former Work:** Engineer
**FI/FIRE Age:** Thirties
**Source/FI Accelerator:** Stock
Investments

**Name:** Adam (Minafi)
**Former Work:** Engineer
**FI/FIRE Age:** Thirty-Six
**Source/FI Accelerator:** Stock
Investments

**Name:** Chad Carson
(Coach Carson)
**Former Work:** NCAA Football Player
**FI/FIRE Age:** Thirties
**Source/FI Accelerator:** Real Estate
Investments

**Name:** Sam Dogen
(Financial Samurai)
**Former Work:** Investment Banker
**FI/FIRE Age:** Thirties
**Source/FI Accelerator:** Stock & Real
Estate Investments

**Name:** Steve Ark (Steve Ark)
**Former Work:** Chemical Engineer
**FI/FIRE Age:** Fifties
**Source/FI Accelerator:** Real Estate
Investments

**Name:** Jeff (Mr. Hobo Millionaire)
**Former Work:** Entrepreneur
**FI/FIRE Age:** Forties
**Source/FI Accelerator:** Business
Equity & Investments

**Name:** Michelle Schroeder-Gardner
(Making Sense of Cents)
**Former Work:** Blogger
**FI/FIRE Age:** Twenties
**Source/FI Accelerator:**
Entrepreneurship/Blogging

# "CHALLENGE YOUR ASSUMPTIONS, QUESTION EVERYTHING, AND START WORKING TOWARD THE LIFE THAT WILL BE MOST MEANINGFUL AND ENJOYABLE TO YOU."

**Brandon Ganch (aka The Mad Fientist)**

**Name:** Dom (Gen Y Finance Guy)
**Former Work:** Corporate Finance
**FI/FIRE Age:** Thirties
**Source/FI Accelerator:** Stock Investments/Entrepreneurship

**Name:** Robert Farrington (The College Investor)
**Former Work:** Regional Manager at Target
**FI/FIRE Age:** Thirties
**Source/FI Accelerator:** Blogging/Entrepreneurship

**Name:** John (ESI Money)
**Former Work:** Corporate Career
**FI/FIRE Age:** Forty-Two
**Source/FI Accelerator:** Stock & Real Estate Investments

**Name:** Brad Barret (ChooseFI)
**Former Work:** Accountant
**FI/FIRE Age:** Thirty-Five
**Source/FI Accelerator:** Stock Investments

**Name:** Kristy Shen (Millennial Revolution)
**Former Work:** Computer Engineer
**FI/FIRE Age:** Thirty-One
**Source/FI Accelerator:** Stock & Real Estate Investments

**Name:** Jim Wang (Wallet Hacks)
**Former Work:** Software Engineer
**FI/FIRE Age:** Twenties
**Source/FI Accelerator:** Blogging/Entrepreneurship

**Name:** Paula Pant (Afford Anything)
**Former Work:** Freelance Writer
**FI/FIRE Age:** Thirties
**Source/FI Accelerator:** Real Estate Investments/Entrepreneurship

**Name:** Doug Nordman (The Military Guide)
**Former Work:** US Navy Sailor
**FI/FIRE Age:** Forty-One
**Source/FI Accelerator:** Stock Investments/Government Pension

**Name:** Chris Mamula (Can I Retire Yet?)
**Former Work:** Physical Therapist
**FI/FIRE Age:** Forty-One
**Source/FI Accelerator:** Stock Investments

**Name:** Brandon Ganch (The Mad Fientist)
**Former Work:** Computer Programmer
**FI/FIRE Age:** Thirty-Four
**Source/FI Accelerator:** Stock Investments

# CASE STUDY
## FIRE Celebrity Carl Jensen (Mr. 1500)

Carl Jensen reached FIRE in his early forties, and he even purchased a fancy car along the way! So how did he do it? Carl, or Mr. 1500 as he's known online, worked a high-stress software job day in, day out. While he made good money at $110,000 per year, he realized that the stress was killing him.

One day in 2012, Carl decided to hop on the Internet and search for "how to retire early." Guess whose site popped up and opened his eyes? Yeah, you guessed it—it was Mr. Money Mustache. After going down the rabbit hole of "mustachianism," Carl sat down with his wife and came up with a plan that revolved around living off $40,000 per year.

Five years later, Carl had saved up a little more than $1,000,000 in his stock portfolio. This was all he needed to pull the trigger and retire early. He gave notice at his company and walked into a brand-new FIRE life. He was just forty-three years old.

Similar to my own story, Carl's wife, Mindy, is still working. So, you could say that he was BaristaFIRE (see page 16). Although his nest egg was squarely set up to begin withdrawing a steady 4%, he and his wife didn't need to do so yet. And so his FIRE nest egg continues to grow.

What makes Carl's story so compelling is that he fell prey to the traditional consumerist habits that most of us indulge in, and he was still able to reverse course and achieve FIRE.

After living in a four-bedroom, four-bathroom house, Carl and his wife decided to downsize and place the extra proceeds in the stock market. When most people in his position would be looking for a larger house, Carl decided to go the other way. He realized that his happiness wasn't tied to newer and better things; rather, it was tied to his future freedom, his relationship with his young daughters, and his wife.

Carl also made use of a powerful real-estate investing technique called house hacking (see page 110). And it really allowed him to be efficient with his money.

Carl has become a bit of a FIRE celebrity in his own right, being featured on *Good Morning America* and several other media outlets. His writings are as funny as they are helpful, and he's super genuine and willing to give advice. I have to believe that part of this is because he's no longer stressed-out from writing endless code in a cubicle.

> **"THE GREATEST GIFT YOU CAN GIVE YOUR CHILDREN IS YOUR TIME. I AM SO APPRECIATIVE THAT I GET TO DO THAT."**
>
> **Carl Jensen (1500Days.com)**

# When is the best time to **START**?

HOW MANY TIMES HAVE YOU HEARD AN INTERVIEW IN WHICH SOMEONE IS ASKED, "IF THERE WAS ONE THING YOU COULD GO BACK AND DO DIFFERENTLY, WHAT WOULD IT BE?" AND THE INTERVIEWEE SAYS, "I JUST WISH I HAD STARTED EARLIER"?

We hear this time and time again. Why? Because everything in hindsight is 20/20, meaning the answer is clear now that you know the future results.

This should teach us a valuable lesson: listen to those who are more experienced and wiser than us; learn from their mistakes and it will accelerate our own progress.

With this understanding, let's ask the question:

## When is the best time to start pursuing FIRE?

Yesterday, of course!

However, unless you have a time machine stashed away, this is probably going to be pretty difficult. So we may as well start *today*. It's true that there's no time like the present—so take action now.

And before you start to feel overwhelmed, remember that starting today doesn't mean you need to do something drastic. Starting to "take action" could be as simple as making a clear decision to complete this FIRE planner as it was intended. Or it could mean focusing on one section and becoming an expert in that particular area or topic.

Starting today sends an immediate message to your brain. You're letting your conscious and subconscious mind know who's in control. The more

energy we can put into this, the better. We want to build momentum, take action, and then build those actions into habits that occur on a regular basis.

## Not sure? Feeling stuck making the decision?

This is perfectly normal. It's called analysis paralysis.

Sometimes you may find yourself stuck because you're looking for the perfect time to act. Logically, it may seem like a good idea to wait until an optimal point of entry presents itself; however, this logic is flawed. Instead, what happens is that you consistently find something wrong or are too scared to take action. The cost is valuable time.

Instead, practice making binary decisions so you don't need to mull things over too often. Either you're going to do something or you're not. Then at least you know where you stand and can move on to other important decisions.

In order to achieve FIRE, you're going to need to deal with some uncertainty. In fact, you can likely assume that there will be multiple roadblocks along this journey. But don't overthink it; you're far more resourceful than you realize.

So step up now, friend, and let's continue!

# UNDERSTANDING MARKET CYCLES

**ACHIEVING FIRE ISN'T A SPRINT, IT'S A MARATHON, SO YOU NEED TO UNDERSTAND THE NATURE OF ECONOMIC MARKETS IN ORDER TO POSITION YOURSELF FOR THE BEST CHANCE OF SUCCESS.**

Without the knowledge of how financial markets work, doing anything with your money can seem scary. So let's take a closer look at the markets and see how they behave over time. There are many types of financial market, but for the purpose of this discussion, let's concentrate on the broader stock market, as this is a primary tool on your path to FIRE.

For those who are new to stocks, just remember that a stock represents an ownership share in a specific publicly traded company. So if you own a share of DIS, you own a small portion of the Walt Disney Company.

Stocks are listed and traded on exchanges such as the New York Stock Exchange, NASDAQ, London Stock Exchange, Shanghai Stock

Exchange, and Euronext, to name a few. However, you may see them referred to collectively as the "stock market."

Indexes are used to help categorize a particular basket of stocks. For example, the S&P 500 is an index that tracks five hundred of the largest publicly traded American companies. Likewise, the FTSE 100 index tracks the one hundred largest companies on the London Stock Exchange. Have you heard of the DOW or NASDAQ Composite? These are also indexes.

When you hear that the "market is up sharply today!" it's likely referring to a broader stock market index.

Let's have a look at the chart below of the S&P 500 Index since 1927. You can see that over the period of ninety

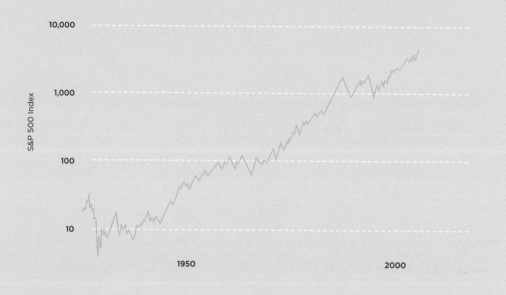

years, the S&P 500 has risen steadily. And the average annual returns have been 10% since its inception.

You should note, however, that although 10% is the average annual return, actually having a 10% year is rare. If you look at the chart, you'll see that there are much bigger swings in a given year, so we want to pay attention to this as we strategize our investing approach.

Some of the most common cycles you'll see in the news are bull markets and bear markets. This is just jargon for illustrating the direction the market is moving in over a time span of months or even years.

A bull market is characterized as positive, optimistic, and growing. It's also used to refer to a point when a market is 20% or higher than its previous value.

A bear market is characterized as pulling back, negative, and shrinking. It's a term used to refer to a point when the market is 20% or lower than its previous value.

# "BE FEARFUL WHEN OTHERS ARE GREEDY, AND BE GREEDY ONLY WHEN OTHERS ARE FEARFUL."

**Warren Buffett**

The good news for us is that bull markets far outweigh bear markets in both length and impact. Historically, an average bull market lasted for five years with gains of 173% versus an average bear market, which lasted only 1.5 years with losses of 39%. As such, many of us invest in the idea that the stock market will continue to rise over the long term.

This is why a large number of FIRE seekers choose the stock market as their primary investment vehicle. They use a simplified approach to investing called "dollar cost averaging," whereby they invest in stock market index funds evenly over time. This way, they don't worry about the ups and downs of the market cycles. Instead, their persistent approach should yield them the reward of averages over multiple decades with little to no thought.

Index investors automatically expose themselves to two advantages. First, they lower their exposure to risk by diversifying their money across many stocks. And second, their annualized returns will be close to the tracked index and keep them in the top ninetieth percentile of investors.

A final comment on market cycles is that a stock market that's up doesn't always translate into a real estate market being up, or vice versa. Each type of market behaves in its own way. The more you understand the patterns of a market, the more likely you will be able to profit from it.

# PLANNING FOR THE UNEXPECTED

**WHEN I FIRST STARTED WRITING THIS BOOK, WE WERE LIVING IN A PRE-COVID-19 WORLD. WHEN I FINALLY COMPLETE THIS BOOK, WE HOPE TO BE LIVING IN A POST-COVID-19 WORLD. HOW WERE YOU AFFECTED WHEN COVID-19 STRUCK? WHAT HAPPENED TO YOUR INCOME? DID YOU LOSE A JOB? DID YOU GET INFECTED?**

If you can remember back before COVID-19 struck, the world economy was on fire. The markets were at all-time highs, and real estate was trading at a premium. Yet who could have predicted a health crisis that would ensnare the entire globe, and the havoc it would wreak on the economy? Millions of people lost their jobs, their primary sources of income.

So how do you manage your finances in a once-in-a-lifetime crisis? And how does FIRE fit in with this?

As we will unravel in the chapters ahead, a well-designed plan is critical to achieving FIRE, and part of this is learning how to anticipate large fluctuations in the markets. I personally did not know that COVID-19 or any major worldwide health crisis would come along and derail our economy; however, I do know that markets fluctuate in cycles.

Remember, we just covered market cycles, and noted that the average bull market is about five years long. When COVID-19 struck, we were in the midst of the longest bull run ever known, at more than a decade. So it wasn't surprising to see the market indexes drop more than 30%. Because I hold a long-term investment strategy, I didn't panic and sell off my stocks. Rather, I added to my portfolio while stocks were on "sale" (see also the Cycle of Investor Emotions, page 101, for more on holding your nerve).

Planning for the unexpected is a skill that's often overlooked. But it's an important tool to keep you in the game. Achieving FIRE means being persistent, and chances are very high that you'll be navigating some volatility during your journey.

So I like to say, "Expect the best, and prepare for the worst." This allows you to be optimistic, and at the same time you can hedge your bets against a worst-case scenario.

A part of your FIRE plan is building a big-enough emergency fund to weather any short-term cash flow crunches. How did you fare this time around? What did you learn from this experience?

Also, don't discount your resourcefulness. Yes, it's nice to have a fat emergency fund to ride out an unexpected life event. And even better is finding a way to thrive inside a crisis by creating value.

I was happy to observe people creating new streams of income while out of their normal jobs. I've seen people starting businesses from home—making masks and selling baked goods, for example. In all cases, these individuals are adding value and being compensated in the process.

# "PUT YOUR LIFE IN SERVICE TO YOUR VALUES RATHER THAN PUTTING YOUR TIME IN SERVICE TO MONEY."

**VICKI ROBIN,**
*Your Money or Your Life\**

*\**Your Money or Your Life** was one of the earliest books to discuss choices with your money as they relate to time.

**MONEY** *beliefs*

*Aligning* **ACTIONS**

# 2

## THE

## FIRE

## *Mindset*

# MONEY *beliefs*

## IT ALL STARTS WITH YOUR MONEY MINDSET

**DON'T SKIP THIS PART OF THE BOOK. BUILDING A PROPER MONEY MINDSET IS ESSENTIAL TO ACHIEVING FIRE. IN FACT, I BELIEVE IT'S THE NUMBER ONE REASON MOST PEOPLE DON'T ACHIEVE IT.**

You are more than capable of physically doing what it takes to achieve FIRE, but do you have what it takes to mentally see it through? What happens when the going gets tough, or fear slips in? Are you confident enough to stay invested in the market while it's crashing all around you?

As a financial coach, I see this time and time again. When my clients come to see me, they're perplexed as to why they haven't succeeded in the past, and they wonder why they fall back into the same patterns and habits.

What they don't realize is that the odds were always stacked against them because they didn't know how to shift their money mindset first.

Your money mindset is a set of established beliefs around money as it relates to you. It's best described as a combination of empowering and limiting beliefs. These beliefs can be conscious, or they can live hidden in your subconscious. Either way, they affect you greatly.

Getting insight into your money mindset gives you clarity. And with

clarity come new choices: Do you like what you see? Is your money mindset serving you, or is it harming you? You get to decide what money means to you. We'll discuss these beliefs in detail in the upcoming sections and learn how to get control of our thoughts.

Next, what does your money mindset believe about FIRE? Do you believe it's possible to achieve FIRE?

Whatever the case may be, you're going to have the opportunity to shine a light on your money beliefs, write them out, and get a clear picture of what your money mindset looks like.

Only then will you be able to shape your money mindset and choose which beliefs you'll need for an effective FIRE journey.

Let's get started.

## " WHETHER YOU THINK YOU CAN OR THINK YOU CAN'T, YOU'RE RIGHT."
**Henry Ford**

# BELIEFS—THE HIDDEN REASON YOU DO ANYTHING

Consider Bobby, a young boy who was born into poverty. His mother and father both worked long hours doing manual labor. Each evening they'd come home exhausted, but they'd still take the time to have a family dinner. During the meal, the father would tell Bobby, "If you want to get ahead in life, you'll have to work harder and faster than anyone else; money doesn't grow on trees."

Now let's consider Janice. She's the same age as Bobby, but her life circumstances are different. Her father was an entrepreneur and her mother an executive at a large company. During their meals, her father might say, "Sweetie, what did you learn today in school? Remember that fundraiser you just did? Learn all you can, because raising money is a great skill to have when you want to start your own business."

Wouldn't you agree that Bobby's money mindset is going to be very different from Janice's? Probably, right? Unless Bobby encounters an external influence that can shift his reference points, his money beliefs will be built on his experiences, and chances are high that Bobby's money mindset will be limiting. On the other hand, Janice's money mindset will be empowering.

What's the truth, though? Both kids are fully capable of becoming financially independent, yet we intrinsically know that Janice holds the advantage.

This is why it's so important to know what your money mindset looks like before you start on your path to FIRE.

Your money mindset is a combination of beliefs that guide you. And beliefs are nothing more than having confidence in a particular statement or story you tell yourself. If you know what beliefs make up your money mindset, then you can predict, with a reasonable degree of accuracy, your future outcome.

And here's why beliefs are so powerful: beliefs are the hidden reason we do anything. They control our actions because we believe that by doing something (or not) it will provide a specific result.

Remember that our money mindset can be made up of both empowering and limiting beliefs. So what happens if you have contradictory beliefs? This can happen without your even realizing it, and in this case the belief with the strongest references will almost always win out over the weaker belief.

Beliefs will ebb and flow throughout your lifetime. But if you're aware that they're there, then you can make a conscious effort to direct or even change them.

# BELIEFS > ACTIONS > RESULTS

# MONEY BELIEFS
## *Which ones are yours?*

**NOW THAT YOU UNDERSTAND HOW BELIEFS DICTATE YOUR ACTIONS, LET'S HAVE A LOOK AT YOUR CURRENT MONEY BELIEFS.**

Sometimes we intellectually know something, but we still internalize a belief in our subconscious. What do your current financial results tell you about your existing money beliefs?

Do any of the beliefs listed below and on page 38 resonate with you on some level? Check all the beliefs you hold about money, and try to be perfectly honest with yourself.

The chances are good that after you've completed this exercise you may find you have a mixture of limiting and empowering beliefs. Which beliefs are stronger overall?

## ⊗ MONEY BELIEFS THAT LIMIT YOU

- ✖ I'm not all about money
- ✖ My friends and family won't like me if I have a lot of money
- ✖ I'm not good with money
- ✖ I can't hold on to money—any money that comes in always goes back out
- ✖ Money is the root of all evil
- ✖ I value people over money
- ✖ It takes money to make money
- ✖ More money equals more problems
- ✖ I don't deserve to have a lot of money
- ✖ Money is not that important
- ✖ The rich get richer and the poor get poorer
- ✖ I can't save money

- ✖ My net worth is a reflection of my self-worth. I'm not destined to be rich
- ✖ To make money you need to take some risks
- ✖ Money can't buy happiness
- ✖ I can't be rich when other people are so poor
- ✖ It's selfish and greedy to want a lot of money
- ✖ It's only money (i.e., money is not that important)
- ✖ I don't have enough to give
- ✖ I don't have enough time to focus on money
- ✖ FIRE is a cool concept, but it's not something I could ever achieve
- ✖ I don't have enough income to save for FIRE

# Add your own limiting beliefs . . .

# ✅ MONEY BELIEFS THAT EMPOWER YOU

✓ Money doesn't define who I am

✓ My friends and family like when I have money because I always have a smile on my face, and it encourages me to do kind things

✓ I'm great with money

✓ I'm a money magnet—money sticks to me like glue

✓ The "pursuit" of money is the root of all evil; I pursue freedom and authenticity

✓ I know that valuing people and valuing money are not mutually exclusive

✓ It takes creativity and persistence to create streams of income

✓ More money doesn't eliminate problems, but most are quality ones (such as I'm paying too much in taxes because my income is so high)

✓ I deserve to have a lot of money because I know that I will steward it for good

✓ Money is important because it supports the best version of myself

✓ The richer I become, the more I will help the poor

✓ My net worth is a reflection of my efforts

✓ I'm destined to be rich

✓ To make money, I must consistently believe that I can

✓ Money is simply a tool. I choose to build and create with it

✓ I can save money easily

✓ I will be rich because others depend on me

✓ It's selfish and greedy to not want a lot of money because I'm limiting my own potential

✓ Money is an important tool to master both for myself and my loved ones

✓ I always have enough to give

✓ I have more than enough time to focus on what matters most. If I master money, my life will become richer on all levels

✓ With enough time I know I can master money

✓ FIRE is a cool concept. I'm committed to reaching it and expressing my potential in new ways

✓ I know that with enough creativity and persistence I can save much more than I ever thought possible

*Add your own empowering beliefs . . .*

# HOW TO CHANGE A LIMITING MONEY BELIEF

**NOW THAT YOU'VE UNCOVERED YOUR LIMITING MONEY BELIEFS, THE MILLION-DOLLAR QUESTION IS: HOW DO YOU CHANGE A LIMITING BELIEF INTO AN EMPOWERING ONE?**

A deep-seated belief typically comes from a moment of high emotion, followed by a strong set of reference points to reinforce that particular story.

Let's take a common limiting belief from the list. Debbie believes, "I'm not destined to be rich."

When she was just ten, she tried to play with a group of girls at school. However, she was devastated when one of the girls told her, "Look at your clothes. You can never play with us because poor girls have to play with poor girls." This was the first time she realized she was different, and it hurt.

This limiting belief may have been backed up further by:

- Growing up in a poorer neighborhood

- Never having money to buy proper clothes or nice things

- Hearing her parents tell her, "We'll never be rich."

These are strong reference points that hold up this belief. But you can override these reference points by creating or finding new ones.

Inspiration is one of the best tools I know of to shift a belief. What if you found someone who came from a similar background who *did* escape and become rich? What if you read books by authors who came from nothing and now own businesses and real estate? Wouldn't that make you think that if they can do it, then maybe you can too?

The good news is that you can reprogram your mind to tell it what to think. Our brains are like computers. Whatever goes in is what ultimately comes out. So let's look at affirmations and incantations.

An affirmation is a statement or belief that you say out loud, like "I can make a lot of money by being resourceful." Your brain is forced to listen to it, and it starts to believe what you're saying. Even more powerful is an incantation: taking an affirmation and injecting peak energy into it. Try it out. When you say, "I can make a lot of money by being resourceful," say it super loud and beat your chest while you do it. It's a different experience, and your subconscious has no choice but to listen.

Look, I know that incantations may seem a bit bizarre at first. Your neighbors and family might be thinking, "Who's that crazy person over there?" But what's even crazier is knowing you have a limiting belief and allowing it to remain.

Another great tool to shift a belief is to hang out with positive people who already believe what you want to believe. This is called the power of proximity. Choosing who you want to hang out with is absolutely critical; by selecting a positive peer group, you'll naturally raise your own standards.

What if you don't have any friends who believe as you'd like to believe? You can get resourceful and use technology to your advantage to find an investors' group or even join a wealth creation group online. Or you can hire a coach, or join a paid mastermind group to help find like-minded individuals. This isn't going to be free, but it's an investment in your personal growth, and if you're able to make that final shift out of a poor belief and into a rich belief, then wouldn't it be worth it?

Lastly, education is the great equalizer. The more you learn about a topic, the more comfortable you'll feel about it. So, if you study how to become rich or how to reach FIRE, your confidence will grow and become a positive reference point for your newly empowered money belief.

## Did you know?

Journaling is an easy way to explore your limiting beliefs. Writing for yourself is an intimate space that is yours alone. It's a safe place where you can be honest and explore beliefs without judgment. Ask yourself which limiting beliefs are having the biggest impact on your life. Are they stopping you from realizing your potential? What would happen if you flipped the limiting belief to an empowering one?

# REWIRE YOUR MONEY MINDSET WORKSHEET

Now that you're aware of your limiting beliefs and know how to change them, it's time to have some fun.

**Use this worksheet to:**

1. Rewrite your limiting beliefs into empowering ones
2. Write down which tool or tools you will use to shift these beliefs permanently

**Example**

*Old Limiting Belief*: Money is too difficult to understand

*New Empowering Belief*: With enough time I can master money and make it work for me

*Tools to eliminate old belief*: Education, coaching, and mastermind group

**Belief 1:**

_____

_____

_____

_____

_____

_____

**Belief 2:**

_____

_____

_____

_____

_____

**Belief 3:**

_____

_____

_____

_____

_____

_____

Next, write down who you'll become when these beliefs are firmly in place. What actions will you consistently take? What will life look like? The more details you can describe, the better.

# *Aligning* ACTIONS

**CONGRATULATIONS FOR MAKING A CONSCIOUS CHOICE TO MOVE PAST YOUR LIMITING BELIEFS! HOW DO YOU FEEL? EXCITED? LIBERATED?**

For many people, uncovering and making the choice to change their beliefs is the hardest part of the FIRE process.

You should also know that this process of shifting limiting beliefs is an ongoing one. So don't be too hard on yourself if you have occasional relapses into your old beliefs. The important part is that you can see it happening, acknowledge it, and make adjustments as needed.

As your new money mindset develops and improves, you will naturally begin to take new actions that are aligned with your new way of thinking. This is fantastic, because it means you're growing.

Let's take some empowering money beliefs and see how these could translate into direct action. (It's okay if yours are different.)

## BELIEFS > ACTIONS > RESULTS

## Empowering Beliefs

1. Money is important because it supports the best version of myself
2. With enough time I know I can master money
3. My net worth is a reflection of my efforts and the potential impact I can make in this world

## Empowering Actions

1. You will seek to earn more, save more, and grow your money, e.g., ask for a raise; contribute more to your self-directed retirement plan

2. You will seek to learn more about money, how to invest, how to create value, and you will have the persistence to see it through, e.g., read additional books on investing; join a coaching or money mastermind group; attend investment seminars

3. You will seek to build wealth not just for you but for your family and as a way to help others, e.g., start your own business; volunteer your time to share your knowledge

With new beliefs come new actions. And with new actions come new results!

# MEASURING RESULTS

**MEASURING RESULTS IS AN IMPORTANT PART OF ANY SUCCESSFUL JOURNEY. IT ALLOWS YOU TO SEE HOW YOU'RE PROGRESSING AND GIVES YOU THE OPPORTUNITY TO MAKE ADJUSTMENTS AS NEEDED.**

Let's say that you're planning a very long cross-country driving trip. You know your destination, but you don't necessarily know how to get there. So you consult Google Maps (or your navigation system), which plots out an optimal route for you.

Next, you need to determine the vehicle that's best suited for your trip. You want to make sure it's reliable and capable of reaching your destination within the desired time frame.

As you start up your engine, you should also take note of your dashboard. This is where you'll be monitoring your navigation system and instrument panel. The information collected here will tell you how far you've traveled, your fuel level, your oil level, your tire pressure, temperature, and other useful data points.

By doing all of these things, you'll be giving yourself the best chance of reaching your destination successfully.

Your journey to FIRE is no different. You've already begun assessing your starting point, and you'll use this planner as your navigation system. Likewise, your investing strategy will be your vehicle, your beliefs will be your fuel, and your personal growth will be your oil.

The numbers and measurements we use to achieve FIRE are primarily preexisting personal finance metrics, most of which will be easy to understand. For example, did your monthly income go up or down compared to last month? By how much?

**This month** = $6,000/month vs. **Last month** = $5,400/month

**Increase in Income** = $600/month or 10%

As you track this monthly cash flow metric over the year, you'll be able to take an average and calculate a monthly baseline. You'll want to do a similar calculation for expenses too.

In the next chapter, we'll cover what should be included in your financial snapshot each month.

*The importance of knowing*
# YOUR NUMBERS

**DEBT**

**CASH FLOW**

**NET WORTH**

**USING TECHNOLOGY**
*to save time*

**HOW TO TRACK
YOUR FIRE
NUMBERS**
*with technology*

**THE FIRE**
*equation*

**DEFINING FINANCIAL**
*independence*

# 3

## YOUR

# FIRE

## *Numbers*

# The importance of knowing
# YOUR NUMBERS

ON PAGE 45 WE ESTABLISHED THE IMPORTANCE OF MEASURING KEY METRICS ON YOUR JOURNEY TO FIRE. IN THIS SECTION, WE'LL LOOK AT THOSE SPECIFIC METRICS AND HOW THEY CAN BE USEFUL.

## FINANCIAL SNAPSHOT

**Numbers are your friends. They are honest and will never lie to you.**

Here are some common FIRE metrics to become familiar with:

✓ **Assets** = things of value

✓ **Liabilities** = financial obligations like debt

✓ **Income** = money earned or received from investments

✓ **Expenses** = money spent

✓ **Savings Rate** = (total income – total expenses)/total income

✓ **ROI** = return on investment

✓ **Annual ROI** = rate of return over a twelve-month period

✓ **Passive Income** = money earned that doesn't require active work

✓ **Asset Allocation** = how your assets are distributed within different sectors or types of investments

✓ **Outstanding Debt** = money that you owe

✓ **Credit Score** = score given to you by credit bureaus that reflects timeliness of your payments and other credit-worthiness factors

✓ **Debt to Income Ratio** = how much debt you owe relative to your income

## Financial Snapshot: The Next Steps

Because money is very fluid, it's helpful to take a financial snapshot frequently.

I would recommend once per month in the beginning, and then once per quarter when you're familiar with your cash flow patterns.

A good financial snapshot of your money will have at least these two key ingredients:

1. Your net worth = assets – liabilities
2. Your monthly cash flow = monthly income – monthly expenses

In the beginning, your numbers will be simple. However, as you begin to build up your income and portfolio of investments, you'll want a good system in place to track and manage their performance.

Savings rate will be an important metric to track because the excess money can be directed into other investments that can build your FIRE baseline quicker.

Likewise, if you have debt, you'll want to track your outstanding balances, interest rates, and terms.

Your credit score is another number you'll want to track closely. It can provide valuable insights into your payment behaviors, let you know if your identity is under attack, and get you access to favorable lending terms (if high enough).

In the United States this is managed by a few major credit bureaus that report your payment history regularly. You're generally scored with a rating of Excellent, Good, Fair, Poor, or Very Poor. Other countries have similar systems and agencies in place, although their numeric scores may vary slightly.

Finally, asset allocation is an important metric to be tracked. Assets are anything of value, whether it be cash, stocks, bonds, equity, or something else. Because all assets don't perform equally, and some are inherently more risky, it's good to know how your assets are distributed.

In a later section, you'll learn how to use technology to automate the collection of these metrics and create a financial dashboard.

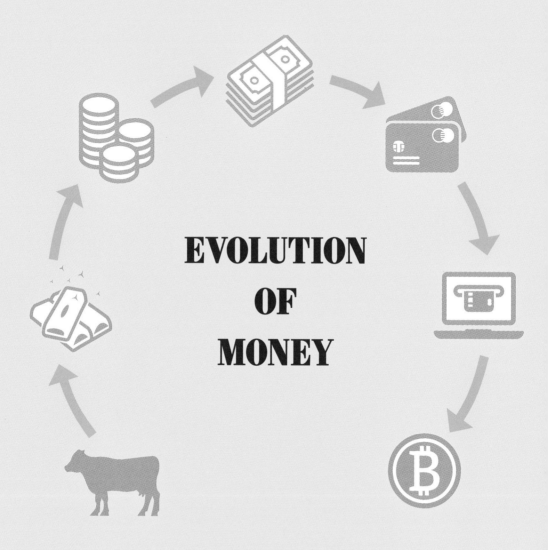

EVOLUTION
OF
MONEY

# THE MOVEMENT OF MONEY

**WHAT IS MONEY? IN SIMPLE TERMS, IT'S A MEDIUM OF EXCHANGE THAT HOLDS VALUE AND CAN BE ACCOUNTED FOR WITH UNITS. IT'S USED TO PAY FOR THINGS LIKE GOODS AND SERVICES. TAKE A CLOSER LOOK, THOUGH, BECAUSE THERE'S A DEEPER STORY HERE.**

Some of the earliest forms of money were animals, shells, and precious stones. From there it evolved into precious metals, coins, and even jewelry. Paper money, or banknotes, only became more widely accepted within the past few hundred years. The latter is called "representative money," whereby the banknote represents a promise to pay the holder of the note something of value. For example, the monetary system adopted by most major countries around the start of the twentieth century was based on the "gold standard." In this system, the banknotes represented actual quantities of gold owed to the holder of the note. These banknotes were much easier to transfer and exchange than physical gold, which is heavy and difficult to carry around.

In 1971, the US government stopped recognizing the gold standard and turned to a monetary system that uses a "fiat currency." The main difference between money and currency is that a currency has no intrinsic value. This is important to note, because the US dollar is now backed only by a promise from the central bank—the Federal Reserve. Most countries have followed suit, and fiat currencies rule our modern-day monetary systems (e.g., USD, GPB, EUR, JPY, AUD, CAD, CNY, etc.). It's important to know this because the supply of money can now be expanded and contracted by the central banks. When the money supply is expanded, you may see prices rise and your money's purchasing power fall. This is called inflation. Sometimes there are important reasons for doing this, like staving off a recession, but others argue that inflating the money supply only creates problems for future generations. Some would argue that it's only a matter of time before hyperinflation—when the monthly inflation rate rises uncontrollably—occurs for all fiat currencies.

It's up to you to decide how much you trust a particular fiat currency. As an investor, you want to maximize the return of value, not necessarily the quantity of currency.

To watch the effects of inflation, many countries calculate a CPI (consumer price index). The CPI tracks a basket of goods to see how much more (or less) that basket costs each year. Therefore, investors look to put their money into assets that can outpace inflation. Examples include stocks, businesses, real estate, digital assets, and some precious metals.

Part of your FIRE journey is learning to assess risk and opportunity. More clarity will help you to make better, more intentional choices with your money.

# DEBT

## DON'T BECOME A SLAVE TO DEBT

**THE CONSUMERIST CULTURE IS THRIVING IN OUR SOCIETY TODAY. CONSUMERISM GLORIFIES DEBT AND FINANCING. IT TELLS YOU TO BUY NOW BECAUSE YOU CAN HAVE INSTANT GRATIFICATION, AND SIMPLY DELAY THE PAYMENTS TO A LATER DATE.**

It sounds like a pretty good deal at first, but is it really?

Be careful. It's easy to fall into debt. When you can't make the full payments, you become a slave to it, and the last thing you want to do is work hard and go nowhere quickly.

Debt is usually created when you "finance" or take out a loan for a purchase.

Let's say that you want to buy a car, but you don't want to pay for the entire purchase up front. Instead, you go to a bank, or the car's finance department, and ask for their best financing plan. If approved, you'll need to provide only a small down payment (typically a percentage of the price) to start. The remaining balance of the loan can be paid back monthly over a specified time period (over sixty months, for example).

In exchange for the loan, you agree to pay back the money you owe plus interest. You are now contractually obligated to pay back the money until the end of the financing plan.

But here's the catch: when you purchase something, you are likely in an emotional state. It's our nature. And when it comes to finance deals, you may overlook some of the details or not take the time to understand the full terms.

While a few percentage points may not seem like a lot, when you actually calculate it out it becomes disturbingly clear how much extra you're paying over time.

> ### ·Ò· FIRE TIP
> When pursuing FIRE, don't waste money on expensive new cars. Not only will financing cost you in the long run, the car will also depreciate at a rapid pace. It's much better to buy a practical, used car with cash.

# DIFFERENT TYPES OF DEBT

**A COMMON WAY TO ACCUMULATE DEBT IS BY PURCHASING THINGS WITH CREDIT CARDS. CREDIT CARDS ALLOW YOU TO PURCHASE SOMETHING NOW, WITH THE UNDERSTANDING THAT YOU'LL NEED TO PAY IT BACK LATER.**

Let's say you want to purchase some furniture that costs $1,000. You pay for it with your credit card and you get to take it home. The credit card company will note that you owe them $1,000 for the purchase. And at the end of your monthly cycle, you'll receive a credit card statement showing your balance due.

If you pay the credit card off in full by the due date, meaning you pay the entire $1,000 back to the credit card company, you pay no interest. However, if you don't have enough funds or choose not to pay them back right away, you have the option to pay a minimum balance and finance the rest. If you choose the finance option, you'll need to pay the credit card company interest (typically very high) on the outstanding balance.

Here's the problem: if you start to carry a balance and pay only the minimum each month, you begin to dig yourself a huge hole that's hard to climb out of. And the scariest part in this equation is that the interest rates can be enormous—we're talking about double-digit rates!

Outside of credit cards, debt can also be used to finance university tuition and expenses, a home loan, and even medical expenses.

Don't become a slave to consumer debt. This is the fast track to dousing your FIRE journey prematurely.

If you're already in debt, we'll discuss some ways you can get yourself out in the most efficient way possible. It may be tough for a bit, but you can do it.

## Did you know?

Once you establish great credit and routinely pay off your credit cards every month, you may find yourself venturing into a popular activity among FIRE aficionados called Travel Rewards. This is strategically opening credit cards so you can earn and maximize free bonuses and rewards. Rewards worth $500 to $1,000 are common.

# DEBT ELIMINATION STRATEGIES & MOMENTUM

**SO YOU WANT TO AVOID CONSUMER DEBT, BUT WHAT IF YOU'RE ALREADY IN DEBT? WE'RE GOING TO REVIEW SOME STRATEGIES TO GET YOU OUT.**

It may take you longer to reach FIRE, but it can be done. And one of the best side effects of this process is that you'll be creating the exact habits you'll need to save and invest aggressively once your debt is paid off. There is great power in building this momentum.

When dealing with debt, you want to have a close look at the terms and interest rates you're paying. You may be tied to several different types of debt, each of which will behave a little differently, so you want to take a strategic approach to ensure the most efficient elimination of your debt.

Personal finance experts champion a few debt elimination strategies (see below) that make a lot of sense when dealing with a series of debts.

Also look for other resources to help you. There are nonprofit credit counseling agencies that can assist you with debt management plans and free online calculators and apps to help determine your debt payoff schedule or target date.

**DEBT SNOWBALL:** You concentrate on paying off the smallest debt first while paying the minimum on the others; then you take the amount you had been paying and move that into the next largest debt; rinse and repeat.

**DEBT AVALANCHE:** Focus on paying off the debt with the highest interest rate first, while still paying the minimum on the others; then go on to pay off the debt with the next highest interest rate; rinse and repeat.

**DEBT CONSOLIDATION:** Sometimes you'll have an opportunity (via balance transfer cards or personal loans) to combine some or all of your debts into a single debt with a lower interest rate. This typically has a limited time window before moving to a higher rate, so use the time wisely to reposition yourself.

**Focus on
balance size**

SMALL DEBT

MEDIUM DEBT

LARGE DEBT

HIGH INTEREST RATE

MEDIUM INTEREST RATE

LOW INTEREST
RATE

**Focus on
interest rate**

# CASH FLOW

## INCOME

**INCOME IS MONEY THAT'S RECEIVED FROM ACTIVE WORK OR PASSIVE ACTIVITIES.**

It's the lifeblood of our FIRE journeys, and yet many of us are never taught to think outside of a primary job to create income.

Common advice will tell you to go to school, get good grades, and find a "great job." Your job will be the basis of your career and provide the primary source of income to fuel your lifestyle. Along the way, you might earn more responsibility, get raises, and achieve higher positions within your company.

Yet with this type of income model you're placing all your "eggs" in one basket. That means if you were ever to be laid off, fired, or unable to work, your income would end simultaneously.

What I learned from my rich uncles was that wealth usually isn't created with a single source of income. In fact, it's much better to create multiple streams of income that don't require your presence. That's right: create multiple streams of passive income!

**Here are some income sources for you to consider:**

- Your primary job
- Your secondary job
- Savings interest
- Stock dividends
- Passive business income
- Rental income
- Royalties
- Side hustle income

Active income is money that you earn from performing a job or service. It requires your time or presence to generate it.

Passive income is money that's earned from sources that don't require your direct activity. Interest income from a savings account is a completely passive form of income, albeit not substantial enough in a low-interest environment. Other types of passive income are better described as semi-passive in nature. An example could be rental income that you collect on a property that you own and self-manage.

As a student of FIRE, your earlier years may be focused more heavily on active income generation and optimization. Use this to increase your monthly cash flow, then take that excess cash flow and begin investing it in assets that will provide you with streams of passive income. The more streams of income you can create, the better. I like to call these FI Accelerators.

We'll discuss these strategies in further depth in later sections.

# HOW AM I GETTING PAID? WORKSHEET

Fill out the cash flow worksheet below. Don't worry if there are a lot of blanks; you'll have time to come back and enter them as you eventually accumulate them!

## How am I getting paid?
Fill out the amounts for each (even if they're $0):

## ACTIVE INCOME
**Annual Income**

**Monthly Income**

**Annual Bonuses**

**Average Monthly Bonuses**

**Misc. Side Hustle Income (Garage Sales, eBay, Home Business, etc.)**

**Part-Time Job**

## PASSIVE INCOME
**Annual Income**

**Interest Income**

**Stock Dividends**

**Annuities**

**Passive Business Income**

**Rental Income**

**Royalties**

**Inheritance**

**Subsidies & Rebates**

**Gifts**

**What is your average monthly *active* income? How could you increase it?**

**What is your average monthly *passive* income? How could you increase it?**

# EXPENSES

## EXPENSES ARE THE COST OR MONEY SPENT ON SOMETHING.

We all have expenses, and no doubt this is an area you're intimately familiar with. After all, our consumer-driven culture focuses on spending freely on anything and everything!

**What are your favorite things to spend money on?**
Financial Independence (FI) occurs when your passive income equals or exceeds your expenses. So in addition to looking at income, it's just as important to understand the topic of expenses.

No matter how much income you produce, if you don't have control over your expenses, you will never build wealth. And an advantage of controlling expenses is that we can make an immediate impact versus income-generating activities, which may take time to yield results.

In a later section we'll discuss the concept of extreme savings and relative frugality as a tool to accelerate your path to FI, but for now let's think back to some of those beliefs that you held in your money mindset. Did you have any limiting ones when it came to expenses?

Many times a client will tell me an expense is "necessary." But the truth is that "necessary" is usually tied to a belief instead of reality.

What we actually "need" to survive is surprisingly small compared to what we actually spend as consumers. Most expenses are, in fact, "discretionary," meaning that they aren't required for our survival.

This doesn't mean you should eliminate all discretionary expenses, but it will be advantageous to become very intentional with your spending.

**Fill out your past month's expenses.**
Also, record a score of 1 to 5 (1 being absolutely necessary and 5 being completely discretionary) next to it.

E.g., Rent: $1,000, 1 (absolutely necessary)

Rent _____

Mortgage _____

Repairs & Maintenance _____

Property Taxes _____

Groceries _____

Dining Out _____

Utilities _____

Water _____

Electricity _____

Gas _____

Trash/Sewage _____

Internet _____

Phone Service _____

Transportation _____

Car Payment _____

Fuel _____

Car Maintenance & Repairs _____

Mass Transit _____

Medical _____

Copayments _____

Elective Procedures _____

Medication _____

Insurance _____

Medical Insurance _____

Disability Insurance _____

Life Insurance _____

Home/Renters Insurance _____

Personal _____

ATM Withdrawals _____

Childcare _____

Pet Care _____

Bath & Toiletries _____

Education _____

Gifts (Holiday/Birthday) _____

Toys _____

Technology _____

Miscellaneous _____

Recreation/Entertainment _____

Gym Dues _____

Movie Tickets _____

Vacations _____

Saving _____

Investing _____

Charity _____

Donations _____

Debt Payments _____

Car Payment _____

Student Loans _____

Personal Loans _____

Miscellaneous _____

**What did you learn about your spending over the past month?**

_____

_____

_____

_____

_____

**Are there any expenses you didn't realize you were still paying for?**

_____

_____

_____

_____

**Are there some areas where it would be relatively easy to cut spending?**

_____

_____

_____

_____

# NET WORTH

## DEFINITION & EQUATION

**NET WORTH, ALONG WITH CASH FLOW, IS ONE OF THE MOST IMPORTANT FIRE METRICS YOU'LL USE TO MEASURE YOUR PROGRESS.**

Just because you own millions of dollars' worth of property doesn't necessarily mean you're a millionaire. What if you owe more money than the property is worth? The best way to find out is to understand the concept of net worth.

Net Worth = Assets – Liabilities

Net worth is the value of everything you own, minus the value of what you owe. Let's use an example to illustrate this.

John owns:

**ASSETS**
House: $250,000
Stock portfolio: $150,000
Cash savings account: $20,000
Car: $12,000

Total: $432,000

**LIABILITIES**
Student loan: $80,000
Mortgage/Home loan: $100,000
Car loan: $6,000
Credit card debt: $1,000

Total: $187,000

**NET WORTH: $432,000 – $187,000 = $245,000**

### What affects net worth?

In John's case, he now knows his net worth is $245,000. But what will it look like next year? If you look back at cash flow (see page 56), you may see the close relationship these two metrics have. What will happen if his cash flow for the year goes up and he invests more money? What happens if he makes a conscious effort to save more? Will that have a positive or negative affect on his net worth?

Remember the movement of money and markets? Real estate values and the value of John's stock portfolio are not static. They can rise and fall with what's happening in the marketplace. Yet although fluctuations may occur, most FIRE seekers are long-term investors, and you want to make the assumption that values will generally rise over a period of time.

# WHAT'S MY NET WORTH? WORKSHEET

**How am I getting paid?**
Fill out the values for each
(even if they're $0):

## ASSETS
Cash/Savings:

_____

Real Estate (Home):

_____

Real Estate (Income Property):

_____

Retirement Account 1:

_____

Retirement Account 2:

_____

Retirement Account 3:

_____

Retirement Account 4:

_____

Business Equity:

_____

Auto/Car:

_____

Other/Misc:

_____

TOTAL:

_____

## LIABILITIES
Student Loan:

_____

Auto/Car Loan:

_____

Mortgage/Home Loan:

_____

Other Real Estate/Property Loan:

_____

Business Loans:

_____

Other/Misc:

_____

TOTAL:

_____

**What are three ways you can increase
your net worth this coming year?**

_____

_____

_____

**What's something new that you can
do to add additional value to your
net worth?**

_____

_____

_____

_____

**Your Net Worth = Assets – Liabilities**

Net Worth = _____ – _____ = _____

# USING TECHNOLOGY
*to save time*

**TECHNOLOGY CAN BE A FANTASTIC FIRE TOOL TO HELP YOU BECOME MORE EFFICIENT WITH BOTH YOUR TIME AND YOUR MONEY.**

When I was growing up, I remember my parents paying for things with cash and checks. Back then, credit cards were a novelty and were processed manually.

Fast-forward to today and you'll find most transactions are processed digitally. You go to a store, hand them a credit/debit card, complete the transaction, and leave. Or you stay in the comfort of your own home and buy your products online. Thanks to technology, buying and selling are more efficient, and the transaction time is faster than ever.

As an investor and a saver, you can use technology to your advantage. Here are a few ways that it can help:

1. **Digitize your financial statements, bills, and receipts.** The less clutter you have on your desk at home, the better. I would recommend investing in a desktop scanner that features duplex (both-side) scanning. By scanning your documents physically, you can file them away permanently without taking up space. More important, it will speed up the process when you need to assemble these documents (e.g., taxes, home purchase, etc.).

2. **Automate your savings.** This can be particularly helpful if you're trying to save up for your emergency fund or a down payment on an investment. There are numerous services and apps available to help set this up, and you can even do it within your own bank many times over.

3. **Automate your investing.** If you work for a corporation or large entity, you may be eligible to contribute to their retirement plan. If so, it's as easy as letting the HR team know you'd like to contribute. Remember to invest at minimum the amount of any match provided.

   If you don't have access to a retirement plan, you can start your own. There are several financial institutions that will help you to set up personal retirement accounts, and they can also help you to automatically deduct a specified amount each month.

4. **Use online calculators to predict scenarios.** For example, there are savings and investment calculators that tell you how quickly your money will grow. Or there are calculators that can help you to pay down your debts most efficiently. Looking to buy a home? Use a mortgage calculator to determine your monthly payments so you can predict how they will affect your cash flow.

5. **Track your FI metrics**. This could include creating budgets/spending plans, monitoring monthly cash flow, tracking your net worth, and even running simulations on your likelihood of retiring early.

*Did you know?*

While technology can be a great tool, it can also create problems. With social media prevalent on computers, phones, and tablets, it's easy to get sucked into unproductive loops.

Consider using a time tracking app and see where your time is actually spent. You may be surprised to find you have a lot of free time being used up inefficiently.

The good news is that once you've identified this, you can make changes and redirect those efforts toward achieving FIRE.

# HOW TO TRACK YOUR FIRE NUMBERS *with technology*

**TRACKING METRICS IS AN IMPORTANT STEP IN MEASURING YOUR FIRE JOURNEY, SO WHAT'S THE BEST WAY TO DO THIS?**

## Caution

You may be surprised when I tell you that I don't recommend you use automated technology to start with. If you're new to personal finance metrics like cash flow and net worth, I would highly recommend you download a budgeting spreadsheet first. Use this to become comfortable with your numbers and how they relate to one another. Physically writing your expenses in this interactive FIRE planner will help also.

It may seem counterintuitive to spend time manually writing numbers in this way, but I assure you it's not. Writing not only improves memory, it also activates multiple areas of your brain for better cognition. I would recommend doing this until you're comfortable with most of the finance terms we're using.

Once you're comfortable with the foundations, there are numerous technology tools and programs that you can use to your benefit.

## Excel or Google Sheets

Spreadsheets have long been a finance tool for both amateurs and professionals. They can be simple or quite complex, but in both cases they help to organize numbers into useful data points.

I would encourage you to download a budgeting worksheet that makes sense to you. If you don't already have one, you can find my FIRE budget/spending plan on my website as a free resource. This can be opened in either Microsoft Excel or Google Sheets.

In this spreadsheet, you'll find that income and expenses are separated by color for quick visual identification. The columns will automatically add up all your income and expenses and calculate your monthly cash flow. There are separate tabs on the bottom to track for each month: one for projected "budgeted" numbers and one for "actual" numbers.

"Budgeted" just means you're filling in an estimate for an upcoming month(s) and you plan to stay within that spending range. "Actual" means filling in the amount you've actually spent.

Don't forget to take a little time to review how close or far off you were with your actual numbers. This may seem a bit tedious; some of you will love it and some of you will hate it. The good news is that once you're comfortable tracking your numbers with a spreadsheet, you're then ready to automate with dynamic software. Below I've listed several online apps that could help you. There's a lot of choice these days, so try a few and see which one(s) work best for you.

## BUDGETING & DYNAMIC CASH FLOW

Over the years there have been many types of software that assist you with tracking your expenses and managing your personal and small business finances. Most have since evolved to live in the "cloud," and accessing your data is as simple as logging into a website or an app. The best applications are available both ways.

- Mint—popular budgeting tool
- YNAB (You Need A Budget)—detailed and well-rounded
- PocketGuard—budgeting and debt reduction
- Quicken—budgeting and tax planning
- Personal Capital—cash flow and net worth tracking

## AUTOMATED SAVINGS & INVESTING APPS

- Acorns—hybrid savings/investments
- Chime—automated savings
- Qapital—savings app with custom triggers
- Digit—simple savings

## ACCOUNTING SOFTWARE

- Quickbooks—accounting software
- Freshbooks—accounting software
- Waveapps—accounting software
- TurboTax—DIY tax software

*Because technology is constantly changing, you can find an updated list of valuable financial tools at* www.financiallyalert.com /thefireplanner.

# THE FIRE *equation*

**WOULDN'T IT BE NICE IF ACHIEVING FIRE WAS AS SIMPLE AS FOLLOWING A BASIC FORMULA?**

The good news is that it can be. We already know from chapter one that achieving FI is when your passive income equals or exceeds your expenses.

FI = Passive Income = Expenses

So, how do you get there?

First, remember that FI is relative. In other words, it depends on how much you spend on an annual basis.

The easiest way to determine your annual expenses is to track your monthly cash flow for a year. You can also estimate this if you have a good idea of all the expenses you'll incur over a year.

Let's say that you determine your annual expenses to be $50,000. Now we know that FI will occur for you when:

Your Passive Income = $50,000

In order to solve for passive income, let's make some assumptions about how you'll generate passive income. The most common way to do this is to invest in stocks and bonds and use the Rule of 25 to determine how much to save.

## The Rule of 25 (aka Multiply by 25 Rule)

The Rule of 25 is super helpful for those seeking FI because it gives you an approximation of how much money you'll need to save for retirement. To calculate, just multiply your annual expenses by 25.

In our example, you know you'll need $50,000 per year to live on.

$50,000 x 25 = $1,250,000.

This is how much money you'll need to retire on, aka your FIRE nest egg or your FIRE number.

This rule works in conjunction with the 4% Rule.

## The 4% Rule

The 4% Rule is an approximation of how much money a retiree should be able to withdraw from their retirement account each year without depleting their principal.

This is based on research conducted using fifty years of historical stock and bond prices that found the 4% withdrawal rate would not deplete a retirement portfolio in less than thirty-three years.

This calculation also keeps up with inflation, meaning that the amount withdrawn can go up with the rate of inflation over time.

*Rule of 25*

| YOU'LL NEED THIS MUCH MONEY INVESTED | IF YOU WANT THIS MUCH MONEY | | |
|---|---|---|---|
| | PER DAY: | PER MONTH: | PER YEAR: |
| $2,500,000 | $275 | $8,333 | $100,000 |
| $2,250,000 | $247 | $7,500 | $90,000 |
| $2,000,000 | $219 | $6,667 | $80,000 |
| $1,750,000 | $192 | $5,883 | $70,000 |
| $1,500,000 | $164 | $5,000 | $60,000 |
| $1,250,000 | $137 | $4,167 | $50,000 |
| $1,000,000 | $110 | $3,333 | $40,000 |
| $750,000 | $82 | $2,500 | $30,000 |
| $500,000 | $55 | $1,667 | $20,000 |
| $250,000 | $27 | $833 | $10,000 |

*4% Rule*

## Perfection is not the goal

The 4% Rule and the Rule of 25 are excellent starting points for FIRE seekers. They allow you to calculate a clear FIRE nest egg figure to target. However, these rules aren't flawless. There are a lot of variables that cannot be calculated within these simple formulas, so although they should cover most scenarios, there's always a chance that they may not work. For example, what happens if you retire early into a long economic depression? There's a sequence of returns risks to consider.

Don't worry too much, though. Worst-case scenarios shouldn't really matter because you'll have a lot of flexibility once you achieve FIRE. You can always mitigate these risks by lowering your annual withdrawal and/or supplementing your income with a part-time job. Furthermore, you can always be conservative and save thirty times your annual expenses.

# DEFINING FINANCIAL
## *independence*

## WHAT'S YOUR FIRE NUMBER?

Now that you know how to use the Rule of 25 to determine your FIRE number (aka FIRE nest egg), let's figure out what's right for you.

In our example, we determined that you spent $50,000 annually for the current lifestyle you have.

### Spending more

But what if you don't want to spend $50,000 per year after you retire? Perhaps you'll want to spend a little more because you'll be traveling to so many places. That's no problem.

If you want to spend $10,000 more per year, it's as simple as adding $10,000 + $50,000 = $60,000.

Using the Rule of 25, you get $60,000 x 25 = $1,500,000 that you'll need to save in a portfolio of investments.

### Spending less

Conversely, let's say you realize that $50,000 per year is more than enough, and, in fact, you need only $40,000 per year to live on.

Using the Rule of 25, you get $40,000 x 25 = $1,000,000.

As you can see, a $20,000 difference in annual expenses means the difference between saving an extra $500,000 or not.

### Future living expenses

When doing your calculations, consider whether you'll be living in a home free and clear or you'll be renting in retirement.

Did you know that some early retirees choose to live on the move in RVs and even sailboats?

What are some other ways you could potentially cut your annual living expenses so you can reach FI even quicker?

### FIRE & future family

If you have a spouse or significant other who will be on this journey with you, sit down together and go through the worksheet on page 70. Have some fun with the possibilities.

Having kids will add expenses, so you'll also need to take this into consideration. And remember that life spans have been increasing, so you'll want to factor that into your equation too.

Finally, what type of FIRE are you trying to achieve? LeanFIRE, FatFIRE, or somewhere in between?

"THE QUESTION 'HOW MUCH DO YOU NEED TO RETIRE?' IS PRETTY MUCH STANDARD. CONVERSELY, 'HOW LITTLE DO YOU NEED TO RETIRE?' IS EXTREMELY RARE."

**JACOB LUND FISKER**
earlyretirementextreme.com

# WHAT'S YOUR FIRE NUMBER? WORKSHEET

All right, we've come to the part of your FIRE plan that will affect most aspects of your journey.

## What would you like your FIRE number (FIRE nest egg) to be?

For some of you this will be super easy, and you've already set your sights on a specific number. For others, it may be more challenging to determine a specific answer. But don't worry—we'll run through a range of scenarios so you can evaluate and then target a number that best aligns with your plans.

Use your cash flow tracking and budgeting forecasts to set your baseline.

Come up with three FIRE numbers:

1. **A conservative LeanFIRE number—how much money would you need annually to pay for your basics: food, shelter, health care, etc.**

2. **A RegularFIRE number—how much money would you need annually to pay for your existing lifestyle? (Refer to your monthly cash flow and track/project out for a year.)**

3. **A FatFIRE number—how much money would you need annually to pay for your existing lifestyle, plus extra activities and/or discretionary expenses?**

As you consider these numbers it's helpful to imagine the cause and effect of different expenses and incomes.

### EXPENSES

- **Housing**—how would your expenses be affected by downsizing your home? What would happen if you relocated to somewhere with a lower cost of living?

- **Food**—how would your expenses be affected if you ate in twice as much? What would happen if you made your coffee at home versus buying it at a coffee shop?

- **Health care**—if you were no longer working, what would be the cost of health care?

- **Transportation**—how would your expenses change if you no longer had an auto payment? How would transportation costs vary if you lived closer to or farther from work?

- **Personal**—what discretionary items are preventing you from reaching your FI number faster?

## INCOME

- What would happen if you got a raise of 15%, 25%, or even 50%? How would this affect your ability to reach your FI number?

- What would happen if you added a side job or side hustle to augment your income? How could this boost your overall income?

- If you earned double what you made last year, what would you do with that additional money?

- What would happen if your investments earned 8%, 10%, or 20% annually? How would this affect your FI number?

_____

_____

_____

_____

_____

_____

_____

_____

_____

_____

_____

_____

_____

## Your FIRE Numbers

**Conservative LeanFIRE Number =** _____

x 25 = _____

**RegularFIRE Number =**

_____

x 25 = _____

**FatFIRE Number =**

_____

x 25 = _____

Focusing on **FI**

**COMPOUND** *interest*

**DEVELOPING** *new habits*

*Saving for* **FIRE**

*Investing for* **FIRE**

*Real estate investing* **FOR FIRE**

*Entrepreneurship* **FOR FIRE**

# 4

## WAYS TO

## *Achieve*

## FIRE

# Focusing on FI

**WELCOME TO THE NEXT CHAPTER OF THIS BOOK, WHICH IS DEDICATED TO SHARING THE MOST EFFECTIVE FIRE TOOLS AND STRATEGIES WITH YOU.**

Now that you've determined your FIRE number (see pages 68–71), how do you feel? Are you excited to make FI your reality? What new beliefs about FI have you adopted?

If you're a little afraid or doubtful, that's okay too. Sometimes you have to "fake it" before you make it. However, you do need to decide where you want to be.

## DO YOU NOW BELIEVE . . . ?

✓ I'm in full control of my financial destiny

✓ It's possible to achieve FI

✓ Reaching FI doesn't need to take a lifetime

✓ The gifts along the FI journey are abundant and not just monetary

✓ I'm no longer willing to settle for average

✓ FI is my destiny and nothing will stop me

✓ FI is a worthy goal for me, my family, and my friends

✓ I can leverage strategies and tactics from those who have already done it

## Decision can override belief

In the short term, a firm decision can override a limiting belief.

Find some inspiration from the FIRE case studies throughout this book and learn about the mindset these individuals created before reaching FI. It's not luck or skill. It's a choice. And you're fully capable of doing the same.

Make the decision to create an empowering FI mindset. Take action on strategies that have been tested. You'll find that achieving FIRE is well within your reach. And the more action you take, the more momentum you'll build, and in the process your empowering beliefs will strengthen and serve you long term.

## Modeling FI success

Success leaves clues and patterns. Closely study those who have achieved FIRE already and their respective paths. Modeling yourself on others who have already achieved what you're trying to do will cut your trial-and-error period significantly.

This doesn't mean you won't make mistakes, but it should mean you make fewer, and the time you save by using this strategy will be invaluable.

## Find an FI Accelerator that speaks to you

This chapter will expose you to three incredible FI Accelerators:

1. **Extreme Savings/Investing**
2. **Real Estate Investing**
3. **Entrepreneurship**

Which one is in line with your style?

Learn how to get creative within these strategies and make money from ideas alone. Have fun exploring!

## Make success a habit

Finally, learn how to develop FI habits and put your actions on autopilot.

It may seem slow when you start, but this stage is when you're actually doing the heavy lifting, and once compound interest gives you a push, it gets significantly easier to grow your money.

It's time to generate new income, save intentionally, and become more efficient.

Let's go!

# COMPOUND *interest*

## THE MAGIC INGREDIENT OF FIRE

**CHANCES ARE GOOD THAT YOU'VE HEARD THE PHRASE "MAKE YOUR MONEY WORK FOR YOU." BUT WHAT DOES THAT MEAN, EXACTLY? HOW CAN YOUR MONEY WORK FOR YOU? THE ANSWER TO THAT QUESTION IS COMPOUND INTEREST.**

I've referenced compound interest already in other sections, but let's take a little time to dive into it in more detail.

**Compound interest** = interest accrued on an initial balance that is also inclusive of accumulated interest from prior periods.

The easiest way to think about it is that you get to earn interest on interest! This is truly remarkable, because growth upon growth is what creates scale and the ability to generate wealth without additional effort. It's the magic ingredient of FIRE. Let's have a look and see why.

**STARTING PRINCIPAL = $10,000**

**Interest Rate:** 10% Annual Rate of Return  **Time Frame:** Five Years

| | | | |
|---|---|---|---|
| **Today** | = $10,000 | | |
| **Year 1** | = $10,000 | + $1,000 (interest on $10,000) | = $11,000 |
| **Year 2** | = $11,000 | + $1,100 (interest on $11,000) | = $12,100 |
| **Year 3** | = $12,100 | + $1,210 (interest on $12,100) | = $13,310 |
| **Year 4** | = $13,310 | + $1,331 (interest on $13,310) | = $14,641 |
| **Year 5** | = $14,641 | + $1,464 (interest on $14,461) | = $16,105 |

**ENDING PRINCIPAL = $16,105**

Not bad, right? An increase of $6,105 over five years is a healthy return. But the true magic happens when you extend these time frames even farther out. What happens to this same $10,000 investment over ten years? Twenty years? Or even thirty years?

Year Ten = **$25,937**   Year Twenty = **$67,275**   Year Thirty = **$174,494**   Wow.

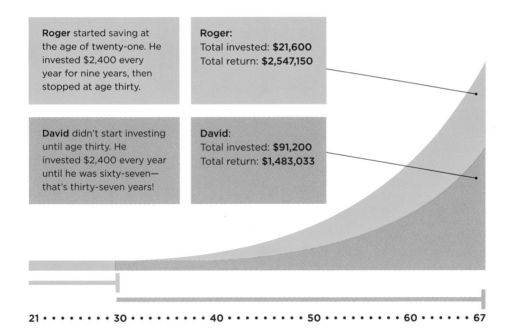

**The moral of the story is START EARLY**

The graphic above shows why it's so important to start now: the earlier you begin, the better. This is precisely how the rich stay rich, and how the poor stay poor.

Compound interest can work in reverse too. Remember the section on credit card debt? If you allow your outstanding balances to grow unchecked, you may find yourself in a hole you're unable to dig out from.

## Rule of 72

Compound interest is awesome, but working it out can be tricky unless you're able to calculate logarithmic functions in your head.

So, a wonderful tool called the Rule of 72 can help you to determine roughly how long it will take to double your money with a fixed annual rate of return.

Time to Double Initial Investment = 72 / annual rate of return = number of years

Let's say you have $1,000 that you're going to invest in the stock market and you're anticipating a 10% annual return on your money. You want to know how long it will take to double your money. So, if you divide 72 by 10%, you can estimate that your initial principal of $1,000 will double in 7.2 years.

# DEVELOPING *new habits*

**MOST OF US ARE CREATURES OF HABIT. WE TEND TO DO THINGS IN THE SAME OR SIMILAR FASHION OVER AND OVER AGAIN.**

Habits help us to get through the day without having to think about everything we do. This would simply require too much mental energy, so we revert to creating habits to serve ourselves more efficiently.

Habits are incredibly powerful because they control many of our actions, and as you now know, actions lead to results.

For the most part, habits serve us well. You get up in the morning and follow a specific routine of habits: go to the bathroom, take a shower, brush your teeth, and get ready for the day. And you can perform some or all of these with minimal thought because they're already habits. It's also fantastic because these daily actions lead to good personal hygiene and help you feel prepared for the day ahead.

We also have bad habits that don't serve us. Perhaps it's an addiction to smoking, drinking excessively, or overeating. While these actions may provide temporary satisfaction, they will ultimately create poor results for ourselves and lead to health complications if left unchecked.

## When it comes to FIRE, there are some key habits to adopt:

**1. Make it manageable**—habits are hard to adopt if they're too complex or require too much effort; better to keep things simple if possible.

**2. Gratification**—you'll be much more inclined to perform a habit if you have short-term gratification. Reached a savings goal? Consider buying yourself a small present or having a cup of ice cream to celebrate.

**3. Habit stacking**—if you need to start a new habit, stack it on top of an existing one. If you already know you're going to brush your teeth, consider writing the new habit on the bathroom mirror so that you'll see it every morning.

**4. Social contracts**—building a new habit can be a social event when you publicly declare a goal. Knowing that others are watching you is good peer pressure.

**5. Pain and pleasure**—we discussed the gratification (pleasure) component of a habit, but the avoidance of pain is another strong incentive to begin a habit.

What are your best financial habits? Could you enhance any of these to create a larger impact?

_____

_____

_____

_____

_____

_____

_____

_____

What are your bad financial habits? How have they *not* served you so far? (There's no judgment here, just an opportunity for honesty in service to your future.)

_____

_____

_____

_____

_____

_____

_____

Effective financial habits don't need to be hard. Which of the following could you adopt this week?

• Review your monthly income
• Review your monthly expenses
• Read a personal finance article every week
• Join an investment club
• Watch a YouTube video on investing weekly
• Keep a money journal

Add a few ideas of your own:

_____

_____

_____

_____

_____

_____

_____

_____

_____

_____

_____

# Saving for FIRE

**NOW THAT WE UNDERSTAND WHAT YOUR FIRE NUMBER IS GOING TO BE, IT'S TIME TO START LOOKING CLOSELY AT THE TOOLS AND STRATEGIES THAT CAN MAKE THIS NUMBER A REALITY.**

Saving for FIRE is where you'll want to begin.

It doesn't matter if you make $15 per hour or $10,000 per hour. If you don't save more than you spend, you'll never reach your FIRE number.

This may sound a bit ludicrous, but this scenario happens more often than you think. Here are some high-profile names who went broke:

- **Michael Jackson**—world-renowned musician who earned hundreds of millions ultimately ended up in bankruptcy and debt before his death.

- **Mike Tyson**—one of the world's best boxers earned more than $400 million during his career and ended up $23 million in debt in 2003.

- **Lindsay Lohan**—top-earning actress of her time earned millions and lost millions once her partying lifestyle caught up with her. She filed for bankruptcy in 2012.

These are just some of the celebrities who made the headlines, but this occurs commonly within our society. So why does this happen? A part of it is down to the consumerism you're inundated with—you see the glorification of spending on TV and in film, advertisements, and pop culture.

## Pay yourself first

One great way to look at savings is to view it as "paying yourself first." By framing it this way, you're placing your savings above all else; you are the priority above all other expenses.

Traditional financial advisers will recommend saving 15% of your annual income. And while this is a good start, your journey to build up your FIRE number will be slow at this rate. We've already seen what the power of compound interest can do for you given enough time, so it behooves you to save as much as you can as quickly as possible.

Saving is easier said than done. You've already begun listing out your monthly expenses—and were you surprised to see so many? It may feel impossible to eliminate many of these, but don't be fooled. This is a limiting belief speaking to you.

The truth is that you're capable of saving a significant portion of your income while still being able to afford a happy and healthy lifestyle.

If you're looking for some encouragement, determine your three largest expenses and ask yourself if these could be reduced.

Alternatively, look at your income and ask yourself if there's anything you can do to increase your pay.

Both options will allow you to save more relative to where you are currently.

Next, you'll want to use automation and pre-planning to allocate your surplus among savings and investments.

# DELAYED GRATIFICATION

**LEARNING TO SAVE AGGRESSIVELY IS A SKILL LIKE ANYTHING ELSE. OTHERS HAVE MASTERED IT, AND YOU CAN TOO.**

Remember the genius of Pete, Mr. Money Mustache (see page 23)? He identified that hedonic adaptation is the tendency for you to revert back to similar levels of happiness regardless of major shifts in your life. What that means is that beyond a certain level of spending, you won't gain additional happiness.

Once you understand this, you can stop chasing happiness through purchases. It no longer makes sense to do so. Why would you continue buying "things" if you already know the reward is an illusion?

## "FOR EVERY DISCIPLINED EFFORT THERE IS A MULTIPLE REWARD."
**Jim Rohn**

The secret hiding in plain sight is that the riches lie in delayed gratification. A forty-year-long Stanford research study showed that people who practice delayed gratification are more likely to succeed. This is applicable to FIRE and money, and also to health and overall well-being. Look around you. Who do you view as successful? Have they used delayed gratification to achieve a result you admire?

Learning to save may feel uncomfortable at first. That's okay. In fact, it's great! It means that you're growing and training yourself to invest in your future. Over time, it will feel less and less uncomfortable, and if you employ automation in your savings strategy, you don't even need to think about it. The habit will be set, and your momentum to achieve your FIRE number will be in place.

## "GREAT INVESTING REQUIRES A LOT OF DELAYED GRATIFICATION."
**Charlie Munger**

Remember our cross-country car example? What kind of car do you want to drive? Do you want extra comfort even if it means a slower ride? Or do you want the lightest, no-frills speedster that can get you there the fastest?

## Cutting excess

Sometimes you completely forget how much you're paying for something. Consider delaying some of your gratification in these areas:

- "Cut the cord"—cut out cable and stick to free Internet programming
- Participate in a "No Spend" monthly challenge
- Sell off unnecessary "stuff"
- Downsize your living accommodations
- Move to an area with a lower cost of living
- Live in an RV
- Eliminate one or all of your cars
- Buy items used or open-box
- Eliminate or minimize eating out
- Eliminate drink purchases from retail stores
- Grow your own food

How much can you feasibly save each month?

_____

_____

_____

_____

# INTENTIONAL SPENDING

**DELAYING GRATIFICATION NATURALLY LEADS TO INTENTIONAL SPENDING.**

With so many expenses and limited attention, it can be easy to forget about certain expenses and/or remember why you purchased something in the first place.

Intentional spending is the practice of buying with purpose. How do you maximize your happiness with a purchase most efficiently?

## Utility

In economics, we call this term "utility." Utility is the satisfaction you get from consuming a good or service. By considering this, you'll not only receive a more focused satisfaction from your purchases but also begin to realize that certain expenses don't provide as much utility.

## "SPEND LAVISHLY ON THE THINGS YOU VALUE, AND CUT MERCILESSLY ON THE THINGS YOU DON'T."
**Ramit Seti**
*I Will Teach You to Be Rich*

**What purchases provide you the most utility (satisfaction) in your life?**

**What feelings do you get when you buy them?**

Consider the types of purchase you make. Are they mostly consumer items? Assets? Travel? Perhaps education?

_____

_____

_____

_____

_____

_____

_____

_____

_____

**What makes one type of purchase better or worse than another?**

_____

_____

_____

_____

_____

_____

_____

_____

## Intentional spending ideas

- Review your monthly cash flow. Are all of the expenses necessary? What's the opportunity cost?

- Consider spacing out your purchases

- Create a tight budget and then stick to it

- Learn from your past purchases when you've had buyer's remorse

- Identify a cheaper (or free) alternative

## Emotional purchases

Did you know that 95% of your purchases are made subconsciously? And emotion is the number one factor in this. Now that you know this, you can ask yourself better questions to understand your true desires.

Ask yourself:

- Why do I really want this?

- What feeling will I get from this purchase? Happiness? Acceptance? Excitement?

_____

_____

_____

_____

_____

_____

# INCOME ACCELERATION

**PERSONAL FINANCE ADVICE IS NEVER SHORT ON SAVINGS AND EXPENSE REDUCTION IDEAS. IT'S EASY TO FIND CLEVER SAVING HACKS, CHALLENGES, AND TOOLS, MANY OF WHICH ARE EXCELLENT WAYS TO ACCELERATE YOUR SAVINGS HABITS.**

The only problem with saving is that it's finite. In other words, there's only so much you can save before you hit 100% and you can't save anymore.

On the other side of the equation is income, and income is limitless—meaning that you can earn more and more with no finite stopping point.

Some may argue that your income is limited by the time available to you to earn it. However, if you learn to invest or become an entrepreneur, you can earn money without using any of your time.

We know that your monthly cash flow is your income minus your expenses. So what would happen if you increased your income by 25% or 50% or doubled it? If you kept your expenses the same and did nothing else, your monthly cash flow would go up accordingly.

Let's say Gina was saving 15% of her income, as conventional financial advice often suggests. After reading *The FIRE Planner* she decides to get aggressive with her saving and cuts out another 10% of her monthly expenses, so she's then saving 25% of her income the following year. Although Gina could cut more, life would get pretty uncomfortable. So 25% is her current savings threshold.

Next, Gina decides to concentrate on her income. She pursues a side hustle that nets her an additional 15% of income for the year. The next year she does even better and adds an additional 25% to her income.

**Year 0** = Savings = 15%
**Year 1** = Savings = 15% + 10% = 25%
**Year 2** = Savings = 25% + 15% = 40%
**Year 3** = Savings = 40% + 10% = 50%

By making these incremental changes, Gina has been able to lift her effective savings rate up to 50% from where she started!

## Getting creative with income

There are opportunities to generate income everywhere.

Start with your current position. When was the last time you received a raise? Is it time to ask for one? What additional skills can you develop that would lead to more pay? What would you need to do to become invaluable to your company, and in the process make your company willing to pay you more?

And income acceleration doesn't need to come just from your current work. Consider learning to invest in real estate or perhaps becoming an entrepreneur.

There are numerous ways to add to or accelerate your income. You just need to look for them and be willing to serve a need. We'll cover this topic in more detail ahead.

# ADDITIONAL INCOME WORKSHEET

What are five different ways you can increase your income?

_____

_____

_____

_____

_____

_____

_____

_____

_____

As you begin to evaluate income opportunities, consider which of these will give you the best return on investment. What skills would you have to develop?

_____

_____

_____

_____

_____

_____

_____

_____

Which of the five makes you most excited?

_____

_____

_____

_____

_____

What skills do you currently have that can make money (including those you use at work and those you don't make money from yet)?

_____

_____

_____

_____

_____

# GEOARBITRAGE

**CONSIDER THAT WHEREVER YOU CHOOSE TO RESIDE WILL EXPOSE YOU TO CERTAIN COSTS ASSOCIATED WITH THAT LOCATION. SOMETIMES, WHEN YOU'VE LIVED SOMEWHERE FOR SO LONG, YOU FORGET THAT THERE ARE OTHER, LESS COSTLY OPTIONS AVAILABLE.**

Geoarbitrage is a creative way to save money by relocating to an area of lower costs. This move could be within your own state or country (domestic geoarbitrage), or it could be more extreme, like moving to another country (global geoarbitrage).

In Tim Ferriss's book *The 4-Hour Work Week*, he illustrates examples of global geoarbitrage by moving to places such as Thailand, Panama, and Argentina. By living in these countries, Tim had access to a high quality of life at a much lower cost of living relative to the United States. For some, moving out of the country may seem extreme, but consider that the move doesn't have to be permanent. What's more important is that you find an area that fits the quality of life you're willing to accept.

In terms of domestic geoarbitrage, there is a wide range of places to live within a given state or country. You'll have to do some research and answer the following questions first:

✓ Is your job location dependent? If so, could you make it location independent?

✓ Is there somewhere else you could live with much lower costs and a similar standard of living to what you're used to?

✓ What is the effective tax rate you pay by living where you are now?

✓ Where could you move that would create significant cost savings for you and your family?

✓ Could you move closer to your family and reduce your childcare cost?

As you begin to answer some of these questions, you may find that the cost savings could be quite significant. That's why geoarbitrage is a favorite tool of those pursuing FIRE, and for those who've retired early. Let's take a closer look at a specific example.

Charlie lives in the metropolitan area of Los Angeles and rents a two-bedroom apartment for $3,000 per month for his wife and young daughter. Let's assume he has a flexible job that allows him to work remotely. Charlie does some research on different cities with a similar quality of life, and in his analysis he uncovers the following:

| LOCATION OF RESIDENCE<br>Los Angeles, California | | LOCATION OF RESIDENCE<br>Tampa Bay, Florida | |
|---|---|---|---|
| Income<br>$80,000/12 | $6,667/<br>month | Income<br>$80,000/12 | $6,667/<br>month |
| Federal Income Tax<br>(on 80k @ 11.0%)<br>= $8,800/12 | $733/<br>month | Federal Income Tax<br>(on 80k @ 11.0%)<br>= $8,800/12 | $733/<br>month |
| State Income Tax<br>(on 80k @ 9.3%)<br>= $7,440/12 | $620/<br>month | State Income Tax<br>(on 80k @ 0.0%) | $0/<br>month |
| Housing<br>(two-bed apartment) | $3,000/<br>month | Housing<br>(two-bed apartment) | $1,375/<br>month |
| Food | $800 | Food | $800 |
| Transportation | $350 | Transportation | $350 |
| Medical & Health Care | $800 | Medical & Health Care | $800 |
| Utilities | $300 | Utilities | $300 |

### $6,603/month

**Excess** for Savings/Debt Repayment
= $64/month or 1%

### $4,358/month

**Excess** for Savings/Debt Repayment
= $2,309/month or 35%

Wow! Charlie went from barely saving anything to saving a whopping 35% of his income. And we're focusing only on the cost savings from taxes and housing. It's possible that food and transportation costs could also be lower. In today's digital world, it's never been easier to work remotely and have geoarbitrage as an option. Is it right for you?

# CASE STUDY
## Geoarbitrage

Jim is an engineer by trade, but always had a knack for winding up in middle management. After a number of years, though, he realized that he didn't enjoy his job anymore. It felt more like a chore; as though he was wasting his life sitting in an office chair at work.

So he started trying to figure out how to retire early—not because he didn't want to work but because he craved the freedom and autonomy that FIRE promised. It also killed him that time spent working was time away from his wife and daughter.

Jim is naturally frugal, and that helped to set the baseline. He saved 60% of his income. He made decent money, but far from what a doctor or an attorney might make. He was also okay living without extravagant things. In fact, he's someone who actually used international geoarbitrage to his advantage.

After growing a portfolio worth a little more than $1,200,000, Jim moved his family of three to Panama. He knew that his US dollar could stretch much further there, including health care, and he figured he could easily get by on $48,000 per year in expenses.

Let's do the math quickly to see if he's in line with the Rule of 25.

$$48,000 \times 25 = 1,200,000$$

Looks like Jim was spot-on. And following his move, he didn't plan on sitting on the beach all day long. He has side hustles to help supplement his income, with a blog and a rental property.

Here's how Jim is taking advantage of international geoarbitrage:

**Food costs are much cheaper than in the US**—Jim can buy an ice cream cone for $0.60, fresh pineapple for $0.50, or dinner for three for $13

**No need for a car**—it's cheap to take a taxi or just walk to town

**Rent is cheap**—comfortable living accommodations in a fully furnished apartment for under $1,100

**Homeschooling**—Jim and his wife get to spend precious time with their daughter and be a vital part of her education

**Utilities**—electricity, heating, cooling, water, and garbage are around two-thirds cheaper than in the US

Jim has a well-thought-out early retirement plan and has taken taxes into account. He plans to access his retirement fund through a Roth IRA Conversion Ladder (see page 172), which allows him to withdraw from his retirement accounts without incurring the penalties of early withdrawal.

And let's not forget that Jim and his family can always return home to Cleveland if they really want to.

"WITH THE EXCEPTION OF SAVING, LEARNING MORE HAS GOT TO BE THE BIGGEST KEY TO FINANCIAL INDEPENDENCE. IT'LL PUSH YOU INTO ACTION (EVEN SMALL STEPS) TO ALLOW YOU TO GET WHERE YOU WANT TO BE."

**JIM WHITE**
routetoretire.com

# EXTREME SAVINGS

**EXTREME SAVINGS CAN BE DESCRIBED AS SAVING 70% OR MORE OF YOUR ANNUAL INCOME. SOME PEOPLE LOVE THE CHALLENGE OF SAVING MONEY—ARE YOU ONE OF THEM?**

**Brandon**, who was twenty-three at the time, went to work for Google in the San Francisco Bay Area. Instead of renting an expensive apartment like most of his colleagues, he rented a truck and parked it at work. Inside he set up a bed, dresser, and coatrack. He has no electricity other than some battery-powered lights and chargers.

Brandon eats all his meals on the Google campus, where he can also take a shower and even work out. With this extreme savings strategy, he'll be able to save 90% of his after-tax income and pay off his student loan debt in less than a year.

**Jeremy** started with $40,000 of debt just out of college. He followed the social norms of buying a new car and even a three-bedroom home. When he moved companies, he got a raise and repeated the process with a new house, a new car, and no vacations. After three years he finally took a vacation to the Philippines and fell in love with the daily lifestyle. He then asked himself, "How can I do this every day?" Upon returning home, he sold his house, began biking to work, and slashed costs. When he got married, the couple continued saving aggressively, up to 70% of their incomes. Today they are financially independent and travel the world freely.

## Extreme savings—is it worth It?

Are you willing to live like others won't so that you can live like others can't?

Extreme savings is a fantastic way to accelerate yourself toward your FI nest egg. However, be careful not to become overly obsessed with saving. There's a certain point at which the extra amount of time spent saving doesn't make sense.

For example, if it takes you one hour to clip thirty coupons before you go shopping, you need to ask yourself if the savings are worth it. To best know the answer, you can calculate your hourly rate from your income sources. An estimate is fine.

Let's say you're making $65,000 per year and you work two thousand hours on average: $65,000/2,000 = $31.25/hour.

So, let's say that the coupons you're saving are worth $15 for the hour you spent clipping and organizing. It's really not worth your time, because you could theoretically use that hour of effort elsewhere to earn $31.25 or more.

The point is, don't let the labor of saving outweigh the benefit of saving in the first place.

## Raise laddering method

For some, easing into extreme savings may be more your style.

If so, I have an effective way to accomplish this with minimal effect on your current lifestyle. I like to call this the "raise laddering method."

This is best used if you're a professional on a career path that includes growth of responsibility and compensation, and it's the method that I used to increase my savings rate up to 50% with relative ease.

For many of us, our first job adds a significant increase of income relative to no job or part-time work while we were studying. We're going to use this lifestyle shift to our advantage, as well as every other subsequent raise.

Let's say Jenny just graduated from college and has only worked a part-time job before. But she's landed an entry-level position at a well-known corporation, and when she begins, she'll start earning a full-time salary. She's never experienced this

before, and it's an exciting time because this is when Jenny will develop her savings habit.

Jenny already knows about hedonic adaptation, so she decides to set up her saving strategies in advance. What if she takes 50% off in savings from day one? She'll still experience a significant increase of income and will be saving both often and early.

Next, when she earns her first raise or promotion, she takes 50% to increase her quality of life, and she automatically moves the remaining 50% of the raise to savings or investing. Jenny is experiencing the best of both worlds.

What does she do with her next raise? You guessed it. She keeps repeating the strategy, and before she realizes it, she could be saving and investing upward of 80% of her salary without any major FOMO (fear of missing out).

Over the course of your career, it's

possible to have several of these events, which could easily leave you in extreme savings territory by the end. And the best part is that because you never spent the entire raise, you don't feel like you're sacrificing anything.

You're much more adaptable than you think, so raise laddering can help you to adapt painlessly.

## - associ- FIRE TIP

It's much easier to save before you have something in hand. Use this knowledge to your advantage.

# *Investing for* FIRE

## INVEST SMARTER, NOT HARDER

**INVESTING IS PART SCIENCE, PART SKILL. TAKE THE TIME TO EXPLORE DIFFERENT IDEAS FROM THOSE WHO HAVE ALREADY ACHIEVED THE GOAL YOU'RE TRYING TO REACH.**

As you begin focusing on your FI number, you'll become aware of new investment opportunities—and this is great, because you can accelerate the time taken to reach FI with some well-placed investments.

In the beginning, focus on one core strategy, and then diversify into other areas if you wish. The majority of those who have reached FIRE, myself included, used a directed focus on one or more of the following FI Accelerators.

1. **Extreme Savings/Investing**
2. **Real Estate Investing**
3. **Entrepreneurship**

Nearly everyone who achieves FIRE uses one of these strategies.

The easiest ways to invest smarter are extreme savings and passively investing in the stock market. This strategy requires limited skill, but is incredibly effective.

Investing in cash flow real estate and starting a business are worthwhile progressions once you've set extreme savings/investing into motion.

Remember, your time is your most valuable asset. The quicker you can get money into a vehicle that can compound it, the better.

Avoid "get rich" schemes at all costs. There is a lot of noise on the Internet, TV, and in society about how to make money "quick." If it sounds too good to be true, it probably is. Think of these like the lottery: it's technically possible you could win, but highly unlikely.

Investing smarter means learning about cash flow. It means learning about the potential return on your investment, and the associated risk involved. The more deals you look at, the clearer it will become as to which are the best.

## Investing in yourself

You already know that I'm a big fan of personal growth and development. Likewise, I'm a believer in investing in yourself with education, courses, seminars, and coaching. I've spent a lot of money on these services and I never feel like they're bad purchases.

Investing in yourself gives you additional confidence to move forward into areas that were once foreign to you, and anything that gives you an edge to take action and refine your results is a win in my view. I know a lot of other successful investors and entrepreneurs who feel the same.

## Don't have any money to invest?

Start by investing your time. Do what others won't. Go to the library and read everything you can about personal finance, investing, and self-improvement, and you'll begin to see patterns of success within these books. There's always something you can do now.

# TAX EFFICIENCY

**DURING YOUR WORKING LIFE, YOUR NUMBER ONE EXPENSE IS GOING TO BE TAXES. IT'S JUST A FACT OF LIFE AND THE PRICE THAT WE ALL PAY FOR LIVING IN A SOCIETY WITH PUBLIC PROGRAMS.**

Therefore, it's incredibly important to be familiar with your tax situation. This doesn't mean you have to read volumes of mundane tax code, but it does mean you have to pay attention to the basics and know where to find good advice. Proper guidance from a tax professional at the right time can easily save you large sums of money.

Each country's tax system is a little bit different, and even if there's no direct comparison between your own country's system and that of the US, the principle remains the same—become tax-efficient!

To be more specific, let's discuss the possibility of investing with tax-advantaged accounts. In the US there are currently programs available by which you can invest pre-taxed money into investable accounts (e.g., the 401k Retirement Plan). The advantage here is that you're able to defer your tax liability until a later date. Instead of being taxed today, you're investing your money in an account to grow, tax-deferred, over time. This is nice; however, you will eventually need to pay taxes on it when it comes time to withdraw from the account.

Likewise, there's another tax-advantaged account called a Roth IRA. This allows you to place money that's already been taxed in an investable account. This specific program allows the account to grow tax-free, and when it comes time to

withdraw the funds, there are no additional taxes to pay on it. That's a great deal. The UK has a similar program called the ISA (individual savings account), which entitles the holder to all of the profits created from within that account. In Canada they have the TFSA (tax-free savings account), which also grows tax-free.

There may be limits to how much you can place in such an account, such as income contribution limits. In this case, there are other ways to get money into a Roth IRA. One popular method is called a "Backdoor Roth IRA." It allows individuals (even those excluded by income limits) to contribute to a traditional IRA and then convert the account over to a Roth IRA. You'll need to pay any deferred taxes, but you'll have your funds in a Roth IRA ready to grow tax-free.

If you like the concept of a traditional IRA and the Roth IRA, you may consider looking into an HSA (Health Savings Account). An HSA can provide a triple tax advantage in that contributions are tax-deductible up front, assets are allowed to grow tax-free, and you can withdraw the funds for qualified medical expenses without getting taxed! There are some additional rules and considerations with this strategy, but it could be well worth your time and effort to explore further and become even more tax-efficient.

## Other tax-efficient ideas to be aware of:

- **Personal residence**—if you own your home and live in it for two years minimum, you're eligible for a capital gains exclusion.
  Let's say you purchased your home for $200,000 and it grew in value over five years to $260,000. You can realize the $60,000 gain tax-free. In the UK, your personal residence may not be subject to capital gains taxes, as it may qualify for PRR (personal residence relief).

- **Investment property**—if you own a US investment property with gains and decide to sell it, you may be able to "exchange" it using a 1031 exchange. This defers the capital gains taxes and depreciation recapture taxes over to the new property.

- **Self-directed IRA**—you can set up a self-directed IRA to hold assets other than equities and bonds. A self-directed IRA can hold real property, precious metals, or even art. It requires you to use a custodian and there's some extra work on your end, but it can be an excellent tax-efficient vehicle.

- **Grants**—the US government at both the federal and state levels have billions of dollars' worth of grants (free money) to assist specific individuals with a multitude of things. This could be money for college, down payment assistance on a home, starting a business, or even money for childcare. Check your government grant programs to see which are available to you.

- **Loan forgiveness**—if you have student loan debt, look into government programs that could forgive some or all of your loan debt.

- **Small business**—as a small business you may have access to additional tax-advantaged opportunities, such as deducting reasonable business expenses. Furthermore, your business can set up different retirement accounts that allow the owner(s) to defer a larger portion of their income compared to a salaried individual.

*Because some of these ideas are country-specific, and tax laws and programs change frequently, you may or may not be eligible for these allowances. Check your country's specific tax regulations to find out and give yourself the best chance of minimizing your taxes.*

# PASSIVE STOCK MARKET INVESTING

**INVESTING IN THE STOCK MARKET DOESN'T NEED TO BE SCARY, OR EVEN RISKY . . .**

Yet a lot of investors lose money in the stock market. Why is this?

Often, it's about beliefs. People think that investing requires active focus in order to profit, and that's simply not true.

In 1975, John C. Bogle created the Vanguard Group. The following year, the group launched the first-ever index mutual fund as a way to track the performance of the overall stock market—not to beat it. Although the idea was criticized for years, the math worked. Not only was Bogle able to prove a long-term return on investment over the next four decades, he also reduced management costs for retail investors.

The truth is that no one knows what the markets will do in the short term, so trying to actively trade into and out of markets to make a year-after-year return is a fool's errand. But if you know that the stock market is up on average over the long term, and you invest with it, the short-term movements won't matter.

FIRE seekers are intrinsically driven by efficiency. So they're naturally drawn to the simplicity and passive nature of index investing. It requires the least effort, ensures

diversification, and positions you to enjoy significant compounded returns over time—but you'll need to stay the course and be resilient.

On a personal note, I used to believe that I had to "figure out" the markets in order to profit; I did my best as an active investor who bought and sold stocks around value and market timing. Likewise, I've also been a passive investor during the second half of my life. In both instances I made money. But in hindsight, I spent a lot of effort and time trying to time the markets when in reality I could have achieved the same results as a passive investor and poured the additional time and effort into other ventures (e.g., real estate investing or entrepreneurship).

If I were starting over again, I would invest passively from the beginning. I wouldn't try to time the market; rather, I would use dollar cost averaging (DCA) to consistently buy a single broad-based index fund (e.g., VTSAX) anytime I got paid. By buying into the markets steadily during good times and bad, I wouldn't worry about investing during optimal times anymore.

Sometimes it's best to just "set it and forget it." Take enough time to educate yourself on which index funds have the lowest fees and how to rebalance your portfolio, then invest steadily and ignore market ups and downs. You want to be invested for the long term, so you'll need to insulate yourself from short-term news that can rattle your nerves.

**My two favorite books on this topic are:**

1. *The Little Book of Common Sense Investing: The Only Way to Guarantee Your Fair Share of Stock Market Returns* by John C. Bogle

2. *The Simple Path to Wealth: Your Road Map to Financial Independence and a Rich, Free Life* by J. L. Collins

**Remember, invest smarter, not harder. Sometimes boring is awesome.**

# "THE STOCK MARKET IS A POWERFUL WEALTH-BUILDING TOOL AND YOU SHOULD BE INVESTING IN IT. BUT REALIZE THE MARKET AND THE VALUE OF YOUR SHARES WILL SOMETIMES DROP DRAMATICALLY. THIS IS ABSOLUTELY NORMAL AND TO BE EXPECTED."

**J. L. Collins**

## Cycle of Investor Emotions

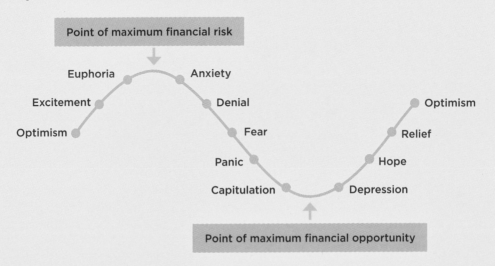

Point of maximum financial risk

Euphoria — Anxiety
Excitement — Denial
Optimism — Fear
Panic — Optimism
Capitulation — Relief
Hope
Depression

Point of maximum financial opportunity

# ASSET ALLOCATION & REBALANCING

**ON THE PREVIOUS PAGE, YOU SAW HOW INVESTING PASSIVELY WITH INDEX FUNDS IS A FANTASTIC START TO BUILDING YOUR FIRE NEST EGG QUICKLY AND EFFICIENTLY.**

Next, you'll want to determine an ideal asset allocation based on your risk tolerance and goals. Your asset allocation is the mix of stocks and other investments such as bonds. Because different asset classes may grow at different rates, you'll want to rebalance occasionally to ensure your asset allocation is as desired.

In general, the younger you are, the more opportunity you have to take on risk. That's because you'll have more time to ride the inevitable ups and downs in the markets. Let's say you're in your twenties and would like to reach FI by your forties. You could feasibly invest 90–100% of your portfolio in an index fund (e.g., VTSAX or VUSA), and leave a small percentage, say 10–0%, in bonds (e.g., VBTLX). By doing so, you'll be incurring more short-term risk (volatility), but you'll also have a better long-term chance of realizing your FIRE nest egg quicker.

As you get older, you may not want to endure as much short-term volatility. In this case, you can smooth out the volatility by shifting a larger portion of your portfolio over to bonds. For example, let's say you've reached your FIRE nest egg goal and are ready to retire. You may decide that your risk tolerance is no longer as high as it was in your twenties. So you shift to a more conservative mix of 60% stocks and 40% bonds. This will shield you from short-term volatility but limit your overall returns.

When you read about index investing and asset allocation, it should make a lot of logical sense. You may even decide to take this approach, knowing that you'll need to weather volatility in order to achieve the necessary gains to fund your FIRE nest egg.

The challenge arises when your emotions come into play during a market crash or correction. Your survival instincts will kick in, and you may be tempted to sell a large chunk of your positions. But don't do it, because you'll need to stay invested for when the markets swing back up. Countless individuals have been caught selling during a low and then clamoring to reinvest when the market growth returns.

## Three ways to mitigate the risks of self-sabotage in the stock market:

1. You can simply ignore the stock market and invest consistently and passively over time without paying attention to the market direction. Basically, you just ignore the financial news completely.

2. You can write up an investor policy (see page 104), which is the set of rules you agree to abide by in good times and bad. By drafting this, you're essentially creating an agreement with yourself to stay the course, and your strategy is already determined well before you encounter market volatility. Your investor policy will also tell you how often you should look at your portfolio and when to rebalance it.

3. You can hire a fee-only fiduciary to manage your portfolio for you. They will help keep your portfolio balanced and manage it according to the index fund strategy you set forth. However, you'll need to do some due diligence to find the right fit. And, you should know that this service can be expensive, costing you 1–2% of your portfolio every year.

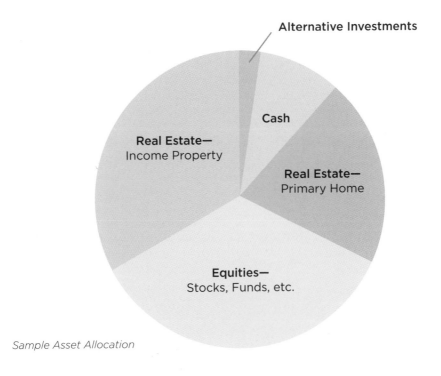

*Sample Asset Allocation*

# INVESTOR POLICY

AN INVESTOR POLICY STATEMENT IS A POWER TOOL THAT WILL HELP YOU TO DEFINE YOUR INVESTING PHILOSOPHIES, STRATEGIES, AND RISK TOLERANCE. THIS WILL BECOME PART OF YOUR FIRE PLAN WITH RESPECT TO INVESTING IN THE STOCK MARKET.

By writing out an investor policy statement, you'll have a tangible guide to how you want to manage your investment portfolio in the long term.

As you now know, the stock market can be incredibly profitable over the long term, whereas in the short term things can be much more volatile, and you'll need to be prepared to weather the storm. During these times of turmoil, you'll be able to reference your investor policy statement and find assurance in your long-term thought processes.

As someone who's seeking FIRE, you'll want this intention to be clear within your objectives.

Here's a general outline of an investor policy statement, although you can obviously customize yours to your liking.

## Investor Policy Statement

**Objective:**
State your retirement target with respect to your age and the size of your FIRE nest egg

**Philosophy:**
Discuss your portfolio makeup, expected returns, reinvestments, and risk tolerance

**Asset Allocation:**
Describe the makeup of your portfolio. Which types of asset are you invested in? What are the ideal percentages of your portfolio? When will you rebalance?

**Other Considerations:**
Describe other investment considerations such as tax efficiency, types of investment accounts to open and when, and other investing opportunities

**Retirement:**
Describe how you will withdraw your assets during early retirement.

As you can see, it's a pretty simple document, and a very powerful one. Another great benefit of having an investor policy statement is being able to add it to your estate plan. If you have a spouse or loved one who will inherit your assets should you die, this will give them a clear understanding of what your intentions were around managing your portfolio. It will alleviate a lot of pressure from them because it's already laid out clearly and concisely.

Here's a sample investor policy statement and a worksheet (see page 106) to get you started.

## Sample Investor Policy Statement

### Objective:
Retire at age forty-eight or earlier through the steady accumulation and growth of my investment portfolio. The value of the portfolio should be equal to at least 25 times my projected annual expenses of $50,000, which is equal to $1,250,000.

### Philosophy:
Invest primarily in low-expense index funds, such as VTSAX, and reinvest any dividends back into the portfolio. My risk tolerance is high. I'm investing for the long term and targeting annual returns in line with the overall stock market, give or take 0.5%.

### Asset Allocation:
I intend to keep my portfolio super simple so I can focus on other FI accelerators outside of my portfolio. It will consist of 90% VTSAX (total stock market index fund) and 10% VBTLX (total bond market index fund). I will review the allocation quarterly and rebalance the portfolio as needed to stay within my 90/10 split.

### Other Considerations:
I will max out my retirement contributions annually, both through my employer's plan (e.g., 401k, 403b) and personally to my Roth IRA. If my salary should ever get too high to contribute to the Roth IRA, I will use a Backdoor Roth strategy. The Roth IRA will be very important later during early retirement. I will also consider using an HSA to invest excess monies tax-sheltered.

If I have children, I will establish 403b funds for them within the first few years of their lives to allow compound interest to work its magic. Should they not use the funds for educational purposes, I can always repurpose them for future generations.

### Retirement:
I intend to retire early at age forty-eight and will require $50,000 of living expenses per year. I intend to have supplemental rental property income to offset my annual expenses, so I may not need to withdraw the entire anticipated 4%. Let's say I need to withdraw 3% annually in early retirement. I plan to use a Roth Conversion Ladder (see page 172) before reaching age sixty, which will allow me to access my retirement funds tax-free.

# INVESTOR POLICY STATEMENT WORKSHEET

Now it's your turn to write your own statement. Don't worry about making it perfect—you can always go in and adjust it as needed.

**Asset Allocation:**

_____
_____
_____
_____
_____
_____

**Objective:**

_____
_____
_____
_____
_____
_____

**Other Considerations:**

_____
_____
_____
_____
_____
_____

**Philosophy:**

_____
_____
_____
_____

**Retirement:**

_____
_____
_____
_____
_____
_____

"INVESTING IS NOT NEARLY AS DIFFICULT AS IT LOOKS. SUCCESSFUL INVESTING INVOLVES DOING A FEW THINGS RIGHT AND AVOIDING SERIOUS MISTAKES."

**JOHN BOGLE**

# *Real estate investing*
# FOR FIRE

**THE SIMPLICITY OF INDEX INVESTING FOR FIRE SEEKERS IS ALLURING AND EFFECTIVE. HOWEVER, REAL ESTATE INVESTING (REI) IS ANOTHER PATH TO FIRE, WITH THE POTENTIAL TO GENERATE SUBSTANTIAL PASSIVE INCOME RELATIVELY QUICKLY.**

Did you know that more millionaires are created through real estate than any other asset class? Andrew Carnegie famously stated that "Ninety percent of all millionaires become so through owning real estate."

Although there is a larger learning curve with real estate investing versus index investing, the rewards and accelerated growth to FIRE can be well worth the added effort. It's not uncommon for those who've successfully reached FIRE to have a mix of real estate investments and stock investments.

Let's look at real estate investing through the lens of achieving FIRE. The FIRE formula still holds constant.

**FIRE = Passive income = Expenses**

Real estate investing offers you another way to tap into passive income via rental income, high-yield interest, equity growth, and more.

## Other advantages to real estate investing:

✓ Tax advantages

✓ Cash flow

✓ Buy right, and it can pay you indefinitely

✓ Property values are naturally tied to inflation

✓ You can leverage the majority of the property value, allowing your money to work harder for you

✓ The management can be outsourced to minimize your involvement

✓ Opportunities to capture appreciation

One reason why investing in real estate can be incredibly rewarding is that you can borrow a large portion of the property value. This cannot be done in the same capacity when it comes to stocks or owning a business. We'll talk more about good debt versus bad debt on page 117.

There are many different types of real estate investing. However, I've selected three strategies that should be of interest to anyone seeking FIRE.

1. **House Hacking**
2. **Cash Flow Real Estate Investing**
3. **Syndications**

## Where are the good deals?

Good real estate deals come and go. Many successful real estate investors set up funnels to screen opportunities and target their ideal prices and terms.

We'll cover this in the following section, but you should know that a good real estate deal should be evident well before you place an offer.

Again, it takes time and patience to find these, but when you do, it's time to act.

*Did you know?*

As phenomenal as real estate investing can be, it's important to be aware of its potential pitfalls too. Like any other investment, there are good deals and bad deals.

All too often I see books or programs touting only the good parts of real estate. But you need to put in the work to be able to identify the real deals. This is why understanding cash flow is so important.

Many times people will claim they are real estate "investors," when in fact they are just real estate "speculators." The difference is that some people will try to purchase a property in the hopes that it will go up in value (appreciation only), but if you're carrying a mortgage that is more than the rent you can collect, that's a dangerous position to be in. All you need is one market correction to be humbled in a serious way.

# HOUSE HACKING

**HOUSE HACKING IS A FIRE SEEKER'S DREAM INVESTMENT. IT'S A WAY TO LIVE FRUGALLY, CREATE CASH FLOW, AND BUILD EQUITY ALL AT ONCE.**

House hacking is buying a residence to live in while simultaneously renting out a portion of it to help offset your mortgage.

This can be accomplished with single-family homes, although many times you will see it done successfully with duplexes and triplexes.

Let's say Larry and Sally have decided to focus on FIRE. They have a baby on the way and are searching for their first home purchase. Instead of following conventional advice to buy a single-family home with a brand-new kitchen and cool gadgets, they decide to purchase a duplex instead. This type of property has two living units contained within the property, each with two bedrooms and two bathrooms.

So Larry and Sally live in one of the units and rent out the other one. They may not have as much space as they would if they'd chosen the single-family home with all the fancy features, but let's see how their decision helps them accelerate their path to FIRE.

---

### HAVE SOMEONE ELSE PAY OFF YOUR MORTGAGE

**Investment Property**

Duplex = $250,000
Down Payment = $50,000
Mortgage = $200,000
Interest Rate = 5%

----------------------------------------

Monthly Payment (P&I) = $1,074
Monthly Taxes & Insurance = $148
Total Monthly Payment = $1,222

**Supplement Income**

Monthly Rent for the 2nd Unit = $1,000

**Total monthly housing expense**
**$1,222 - $1,000 = $222**

---

So income from the rent significantly offsets their monthly payment, and instead of needing to pay the entire $1,222 per month, they only need to pay $222 per month! To make things even better, they can depreciate the portion of the property they're renting out, which gives them access to additional tax savings every year. Furthermore, they can use their savings to make a down payment on another duplex, or invest them in index fund investments. How would you like to have someone else pay your mortgage and help you to build equity while you get to live there super cheap?

## House hacking considerations

As fantastic as house hacking is, you should also be aware that you'll be taking on some additional responsibilities as a landlord and likely the manager of the property. Given how close you live to your tenant, responding to issues should be quite easy. It does take a little extra time, though, so just keep this in mind when you're examining opportunity costs.

## Value added house hacking

Carl Jensen was involved in a different type of house hacking. He purchased a home for his family, and while living there he created additional value in the property by fixing it up himself. As a resident, he wasn't in any rush and could work on the property slowly in his spare time, without needing to bring in expensive contractors.

After a couple of years, with the renovations in place, the home was worth more than what he had purchased it for. He could then sell the home at a profit, buy a new one, and start over.

To make things even better, in the US there's a capital gains exclusion rule that allows you to avoid taxation on your primary home once you sell it, so long as you've lived in it for two or more years (see page 99).

Carl did just that, and even decided to "rinse and repeat."

# INVESTING IN CASH FLOW PROPERTIES

**FOR THOSE WHO ARE TARGETING FIRE, CASH FLOW REAL ESTATE INVESTING CAN BE AN EFFECTIVE TOOL FOR CREATING PASSIVE INCOME AND BUILDING EQUITY.**

Cash flow real estate investing is exactly what it sounds like. It's investing in a property (e.g., a single-family home) that can generate cash flow for the buyer.

Now this doesn't mean you should run out and purchase the first property you fall in love with. You'll need to take the time to do your homework, as it's important to find a property that can generate cash flow even with a mortgage in place.

A quick rule of thumb with which to identify a good property is to use the 1% rule. The 1% rule states that the monthly rent from a property should be equal to or greater than 1% of the purchase price. In fact, some investors insist on deals of at least 2% (yes, there's a 2% rule too)!

For example, if you found a property that rented for $2,000 per month and the purchase price was $200,000, then it would meet the 1% rule.

This is an awesome starting point because, generally speaking, properties that meet this quick rule of thumb have the potential to make it a good deal.

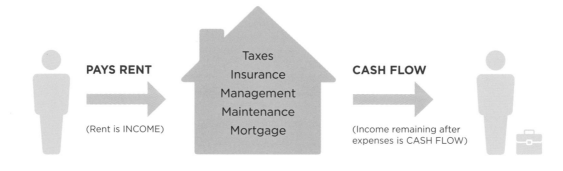

**PAYS RENT**

(Rent is INCOME)

Taxes
Insurance
Management
Maintenance
Mortgage

**CASH FLOW**

(Income remaining after expenses is CASH FLOW)

**Other variables to consider:**

✓ Location

✓ Condition of the property

✓ Vacancy projection

✓ Loan terms

✓ Appreciation potential

✓ Maintenance considerations

Once you find a property that meets the 1% rule (or better), you can then start analyzing these other variables to get a bigger and better picture.

I know several cash flow investors who do well by sticking to certain criteria.

Dustin Heiner (see page 116) focuses on single-family homes that meet or exceed the 1% rule, are located in a specific location, have a low vacancy projection, are able to be financed with favorable rates, and have lower maintenance considerations. Because he has all of these filters in place, he can quickly qualify which types of properties are the right fit for him, and can then ignore the rest.

If you're willing to do the work up front, the payoff can be incredible.

The other thing with cash flow real estate is that you don't need to do deals locally. In fact, I prefer doing deals outside of California, where I live. This is because other states have properties that are much cheaper, and the cash flow potential is much higher. It may seem daunting at first, but if you find the right property managers, they'll take care of your property with minimal input required from you.

# REAL ESTATE SYNDICATIONS

**IF YOU COULDN'T TELL BY NOW, I'M A BIG FAN OF REAL ESTATE INVESTING. THE OPPORTUNITY TO GENERATE CASH FLOW, BUILD EQUITY, AND REALIZE TAX BENEFITS IS FANTASTIC.**

Finding a great cash flow deal can take some time when you're just starting out, however.

What happens if you want to invest in real estate but don't have the time to invest in doing your own deals? Or maybe you're not interested in being involved as a landlord.

Luckily for you, there are real estate investments that can accommodate hard-working professionals—and they offer very similar benefits to cash flow real estate investing. They're called real estate syndications.

A real estate syndication in its simplest form is a group real estate investment. The group is generally broken into two segments, the GP (general partners) and the PI (passive investors). The sponsor/syndicator is responsible for putting together the deal and is part of the General Partners. The GP team locates and gets a deal under contract. Then they market the opportunity to other people to see if they'd like to join the investment as passive investors.

As a passive investor, your only responsibility is doing your own research to see if the deal numbers make sense and meet your goals. And, if so, putting money into the overall deal. That's it!

The other members of the team will work to close out the deal with favorable financing, negotiating the close, executing rehab, and working with a property management team to ensure a smoothly operated property. A good team will be able to meet the goals of the investment criteria, which will mean more cash flow for the investors.

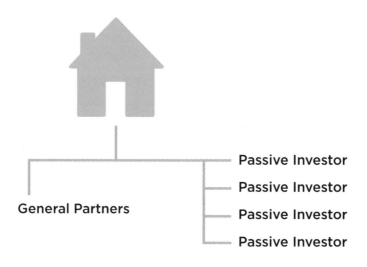

General Partners

Passive Investor

Passive Investor

Passive Investor

Passive Investor

## Advantages of real estate syndications:

✓ Access to bigger and sometimes better deals (apartments, shopping centers, etc.)

✓ Pass through tax advantages (depreciation pass through)

✓ Leverage an experienced REI team (they should bring a deal to the table that you otherwise wouldn't be able to access)

✓ Capital protection (investment is backed by physical real estate)

✓ Cash flow (typically distributed on a quarterly basis)

✓ Participate in appreciation (as a part owner you have access to prorated gains of any appreciation with the property)

## Passive investing doesn't mean blind investing

Real estate syndications can be a fantastic opportunity to grow your assets and FIRE nest egg. However, just because it's passive doesn't mean you should invest blindly.

Like any other investments, there are good and bad syndicated deals. How do you know? By understanding cash flow and learning the structure of the deal.

Syndications are structured a number of ways, so make sure to understand your rights as a passive investor and the fees (if any) that the GP team will collect. If set up well, it should be a win-win for all parties. For example, the passive investors may receive a preferred return before the GP earn their share. This ensures that the GP are working for the collective good of all the investors. If they operate the property efficiently and you're making money, then they should be rewarded.

## Disadvantages of real estate syndications:

✗ Money invested is illiquid until the property is sold or refinanced

✗ The GP may raise money only from accredited investors

✗ Lack of control—if the execution team isn't effective, there's not much you can do other than to express your concern

# CASE STUDY
## REI on FIRE

Dustin Heiner reached FIRE in his mid-thirties by focusing on cash flow real estate investing—and he accomplished the bulk of this within eight years, while supporting his wife and four kids. Let's take a look at how he did it and also understand his motivation for seeking it.

Dustin was a former government employee who worked a traditional nine-to-five job. He was always set on taking care of his family as the breadwinner. However, one day he got a call out of the blue from an upper boss to come and see him. He had heard rumors of layoffs and cutbacks, and to his dismay, his worst fears came true and he was laid off that day.

Dustin can clearly remember his feelings in that moment. He felt like a failure, scared and angry that he was attached to a system that didn't reward loyalty. Yet it was in this time of hardship that he also mustered up the courage to make a new decision. He decided that he would never allow someone to lay him off again, and created a plan of action to become a real estate investor.

He spent $1,000 on an introductory course, and he was off. He learned quickly by taking action and believing he could do it. He focused on buying small single-family homes with ample cash flow. Some homes produced $300 per month; others made $500 per month. He figured out a formula, and he repeated the process until he had over thirty properties creating $8,500+ in monthly passive income.

In addition to creating substantial passive income streams from real estate, Dustin is also proud to be frugal and not spend money frivolously. His family rarely eats out, and they live in a modest house. However, he's happy to spend money on experiences that enrich his children's lives. Dustin's wife is a stay-at-home mom, and she homeschools their children. Because of this, and coupled with FIRE, they were able to spend many months traveling, experiencing different parts of the United States and the world. Imagine the education his kids are getting experiencing places versus reading about them!

After reaching FIRE, Dustin realized that sitting at home wasn't his style. He quickly threw his entrepreneurial hat back on and started up several new business ventures. In addition to real estate investing, Dustin writes a blog, hosts three different podcasts and a YouTube channel, and provides real estate coaching to those who want to learn his specific methods.

**"The most expensive thing you can spend is your time. What and who you spend it on is your choice, but with a J.O.B. (Just Over Broke), you are forced to spend 40 of your 168 hours a week working for a paycheck."**
**Dustin Heiner**
**(SuccessfullyUnemployed.com)**

# GOOD DEBT VERSUS BAD DEBT

**I'VE TALKED A FAIR AMOUNT ABOUT DEBT IN PREVIOUS SECTIONS, SO WHY TALK ABOUT IT AGAIN? JUST LIKE MONEY, DEBT CAN BE THOUGHT OF AS A TOOL. LEARN HOW TO USE IT, AND IT CAN SERVE YOU WELL. MISUSE IT AND IT CAN BURY YOU.**

There's an important distinction to make about debt. There are two kinds of debt: good debt and bad debt.

Bad debt is the kind we've discussed already. It's financing depreciating assets like cars, clothes, cell phones, and other nonessential items, then getting caught up in having to pay it back with interest.

Thankfully, there's good debt too. Good debt is financing the purchase of assets that put money into your pocket.

You've just read about cash flow real estate investing. Once you identify a good property to purchase,

you'll want to factor in financing costs. A good deal will have room to finance a portion of the property and still generate cash flow.

By using the bank's money, you don't need to put in as much of your own. That's an example of leveraging other people's money (OPM) to fund your deals. You can keep your own money available to invest in other things.

Used properly, OPM can be used to help you reach your FIRE number and passive income goals quicker than without leverage.

## GOOD DEBT

✓ Financing an investment property that will give you positive cash flow

✓ Financing a business that can grow and pay you even more

✓ Borrowing money to finance product that's been presold

## BAD DEBT

✗ Financing for an automobile

✗ Consumer debt (e.g., clothes, jewelry, gadgets) that you pay interest on

✗ Credit card debt that you pay interest on

# CREATING VALUE WITH CREATIVITY

**ALL TOO OFTEN WE'RE TOLD THAT MONEY IS REQUIRED TO MAKE MONEY. AND WHILE IT'S CERTAINLY TRUE THAT MONEY CAN ACCELERATE THE GROWTH OF MORE MONEY, IT'S NOT TRUE THAT YOU NEED IT TO GET STARTED.**

Have you ever heard someone say, "It takes money to make money"? Perhaps it was you? Go back and look at your limiting beliefs: did you clear this one out?

This is why I love real estate investing and entrepreneurship. Both of these wealth-building strategies allow you to get creative and generate money out of pure imagination.

## Creativity with Real Estate Investing

One of my favorite aspects of REI is that you can use your creativity to increase the value of a property using little to no money.

**Here are a few ideas you could use:**

✓ Add an additional room

✓ Add a carport

✓ Create curb appeal

✓ Modernize the property

✓ Add solar panels

✓ Add fresh paint

✓ Refinance better debt service terms

When purchasing a property, it can be advantageous to see the potential of the property, not simply its current state.

The success of many real estate investors comes from purchasing neglected properties, fixing them up, and then selling them for a profit.

This kind of creativity can also be applied to cash flow real estate investing. Say, for example, vacancy rates are up, and the property has a lot of deferred maintenance. While some investors may avoid this property, you know that some rehabilitation costs will not only increase the value of the property but also make it more appealing to renters, who will gladly pay more each month for a better-quality unit.

Getting creative with financing can also affect the cash flow of a property. You aren't bound to use a traditional bank to finance a property. Did you know you can potentially finance it via the seller/owner? Sometimes the seller is happy to relinquish the property in exchange for steady cash flow on a mortgage note. This is something you can negotiate with a seller and potentially get more favorable terms than if using a traditional lender.

The possibilities are endless, and there are some phenomenal books on creative real estate investing should you wish to continue your education.

## Did you know?

You can create value with little to no money in entrepreneurship too!

- Design something to sell
- Market an idea or concept (Kickstarter)
- Create a new market that doesn't yet exist
- Improve upon an existing market
- Sell other people's products
- License talent
- Write a book

# *Entrepreneurship* **FOR FIRE**

**ENTREPRENEURSHIP IS ONE OF THE QUICKEST WAYS TO BECOME WEALTHY AND REACH FIRE. ENTREPRENEURSHIP IS THE PROCESS OF IDENTIFYING AN OPPORTUNITY AND PURSUING IT, OFTEN IN THE FORM OF A BUSINESS.**

It's easy to take it for granted, but one of the greatest opportunities in the free world is the ability to create and build a business.

It's true that entrepreneurship requires some courage, persistence, and focus, as without these, it's easy to lose faith when you encounter inevitable roadblocks. However, if you're willing to put in the work and persevere, owning a business can change your life and accelerate your path to FIRE.

As an entrepreneur, there are different ways to bring an idea to market.

1. You can raise a large amount of capital
2. You can bootstrap a small business with little to no start-up capital

For the purposes of this section, we'll be discussing a bootstrapped business, as this is where most people begin their entrepreneurial pursuits.

There are an estimated 30.2 million small businesses in the United States alone. The definition of a small business varies from industry to industry, but, for our purposes, let's say it's 1 to 250 employees.

## The gig economy

The gig economy is used to describe a trend of flexible jobs offered to freelancers and independent contractors. These are often considered solopreneurs, or one-person-based businesses.

Although solopreneurs may not have access to the traditional benefits that full-time career workers have, they have the freedom to determine their own hours, grow, and benefit directly from their efforts.

## Scaling

There are some highly paid gig workers who are specialized and make a lot of money. However, most have limited income because they're still trading time for money.

So, once you've established a baseline of clients and work, consider systematizing processes and scaling your business.

For example, let's say that you run a service business fixing computers. Instead of handling all the sales, marketing, tech support, and implementation yourself, you could make a decision to automate processes to streamline tasks and remove yourself from time-consuming efforts. Likewise, you may hire other people to help with the support and implementation as you focus on building the sales engine.

Scaling is a way of leveraging other people's time and effort, and it can generate incredible profits.

## Selling products

Another way to access economies of scale is to sell products. In this business model, a lot of the work is done up front.

The more popular your product becomes, the more revenue you can generate, and since you've already done the work to source the product and create systems, the additional revenue will add to your profits.

Remember to continue to innovate and support your product's end user for the best long-term results.

## Business liability

Because you'll be transacting products or services with other people, it's always advisable to consider how you'll structure your business. If you start a business selling your services, you'd be classified as a sole proprietor. If you start a business selling cookies with your sister, you'd be considered a partnership. These entities are great; however, they offer little to no liability protection. So, many people look toward creating a business entity to limit their liabilities. They may operate as a limited liability company (LLC), limited liability partnership (LLP), S-Corp, or C-corporation.

Consult with a tax and legal professional to determine which entity is right for your particular situation.

### Small business ideas

There are many different types of businesses you could start today! Here are just a handful to get your imagination going:

**Product-Based Businesses**
- Online retail
- Inventing a product
- Operating a food truck
- Operating a restaurant
- Selling a course online

**Service-Based Businesses**
- IT consulting
- Accounting services
- Food delivery
- Uber or Lyft driver
- Contractor

# SIDE HUSTLES

HAVING A SIDE HUSTLE IS A FORM OF ENTREPRENEURSHIP MOST OFTEN ASSOCIATED WITH PEOPLE WHO ALREADY HAVE A FULL-TIME JOB. THESE INDIVIDUALS CREATE A PART-TIME BUSINESS CALLED A "SIDE HUSTLE" TO ADD SUPPLEMENTAL INCOME.

Side hustles are particularly intriguing to those seeking FIRE as well as those who have already reached it.

They're usually relatively low-risk, because they require limited capital and instead rely on your spare time to run the business engine.

I've run several side hustles since I was in high school, with varying degrees of success. It's a great way to learn about business and hard work, and how to find a market for your offering. And if you can tap into profit and growth, you may very well find that your side hustle offers you an alternate career path as a small business owner.

### Characteristics of a successful side hustle

✓ Can bring in an extra $500 to $1,000 per month
✓ Can be run in spare time
✓ Can be run from home

## Is a side hustle right for you?

How do you spend your time?

What would happen if you redirected just one-tenth of your time each week toward a side hustle? What would you learn? Who would you become?

It's never been easier than it is now to create a business to serve people all around the world.

## Potential to scale

Side hustles can generate some nice ancillary income for you and add directly to your FIRE savings. They're also powerful vehicles for wealth because they have the potential to scale, or grow beyond your solopreneur efforts. All you need is for one idea to take off, and it can literally change your life.

## Side hustle ideas

- Sell food at a farmers' market
- Sell food online
- Resell items on Amazon or eBay (Retail Arbitrage)
- Sell products on Amazon and/or online (Fulfillment by Amazon)
- Run exercise classes
- Tutor students
- Start a blog
- Be a freelance writer
- Become a virtual assistant
- Start a podcast
- Make deliveries (companies like Amazon hire many independent contractors to supplement major shippers)
- Become a photographer
- Become an Airbnb host
- Teach computing
- Provide tech services
- Mow people's lawns
- Paint people's homes
- Shop for others
- Sell art
- Create and sell a course
- Become an Uber/Lyft driver
- Walk dogs
- Help businesses with their social media
- Write a book

# SIDE HUSTLE IDEAS WORKSHEET

## BECOMING AN ENTREPRENEUR STARTS IN YOUR MIND.

In this worksheet we're going to brainstorm some potential side hustle ideas that could work for you.

The examples on page 123 are just to stimulate your imagination. Try to come up with you own, or elaborate on one of the examples as it pertains to your specific skills and values.

**How much spare time per week do you have to spend on a side hustle?**

_____

_____

**Have you ever started a side hustle? Why or why not?**

_____

_____

_____

_____

_____

_____

_____

_____

_____

**What talents and values could you bring to a side hustle?**

_____

_____

_____

_____

_____

_____

_____

_____

**Brainstorm 12+ ideas for a side hustle that would appeal to you. Don't worry about how you'll do it, just get any free-flowing ideas down.**

_____

_____

_____

_____

_____

_____

_____

_____

Who could benefit from your product or service?

Is your side hustle scalable? Or does it require an exchange of time for money?

# CASE STUDY
## Side Hustle

Michelle Schroeder-Gardner is a side hustler unlike most. She's an accidental blogger who actually never intended to make money from her website. In fact, she wasn't good with money at all. She used to spend a lot on clothing and going out, and carried a large amount of student loan debt. Even though she worked from an early age, she didn't have anything to show for it.

**"I had no idea what I was doing, and I thought debt was normal. Everyone around me seemed to have car loans, student loan debt, a big mortgage, and credit card bills. I simply thought that was the standard way to live and didn't think anything of it."**
**Michelle Schroeder-Gardner**

A funny thing happened, though. When Michelle started her blog, makingsenseofcents.com, she met a community of personal finance bloggers doing amazing things—paying off debt, making extra money from side hustles, and retiring early. This inspired her to live a better life.

During her debt payoff journey, she realized that she could actually make some money from the blog. Eventually, she made enough money from her blogging side hustle that she quit her day job as an analyst and became a full-time blogger. Michelle would share ideas that were working for her—money-saving strategies, apps, or different side hustle ideas. This naturally led to affiliate marketing opportunities in which Michelle would get a small revenue share of a sale if she provided a lead to a company. For example, if she shared a book on her website and a reader clicked that link and ended up purchasing it on Amazon, Amazon would then pay her a small referral fee.

Over time, these referral fees began to add up. And as her blog's readership grew, so did her revenues and profits. Michelle has done incredibly well for herself, earning millions of dollars through her blog and reaching FIRE in her late twenties. What's also amazing about Michelle is that she never let chasing success define how she would live her life.

In fact, she makes the business work around her lifestyle and manages to work only part-time. She loves traveling so much that she and her husband sold their house and bought an RV. They toured across North America in it for four years, and have since transitioned to living on a sailboat and exploring the Caribbean, Europe, and the Pacific.

Post-FIRE, Michelle realizes that she's come a long way. Money used to control her, but now that stress is gone and she's able to focus on things that matter to her, which has improved nearly every area of her life.

**"It hasn't been an easy journey, but it's been very worthwhile."**
**Michelle Schroeder-Gardner**
**(makingsenseofcents.com)**

# INTRAPRENEURSHIP

**MANY ENTREPRENEURS FIND THEMSELVES IN THE SPOTLIGHT WHEN THEIR BUSINESSES BECOME SUCCESSFUL—BUT THEY'VE HAD TO LEAN ON A TEAM TO HELP THEM ACHIEVE THEIR RESULTS.**

So who are these important team members? While they may not be founders of the company, they are instrumental players in making the company scale to profitability. And often these early employees are given stock options or profit shares that can significantly impact their income.

These are intrapreneurs, or employees who take a vested interest in the company they work for. They've found ways to contribute and profit beyond their intended job duties.

What I love about intrapreneurship is that it's accessible to many people who are already working in a career. You don't need to take any undue risk by starting your own company; you can simply identify opportunities within the comfort of your own organization.

Of course, some companies will have more opportunities than others, so you'll want to make this a consideration when you're seeking a job. Look for a company that's growing and presents opportunities to its employees.

Did you know that large corporations like Google encourage intrapreneurship? They allow their employees to spend 20% of their working hours on innovation projects that they think will help Google. Many of their best products have come from this program, including gmail, Google Maps, and AdSense!

So, if you don't want to take the full risks of entrepreneurship, consider intrapreneurship as a less risky alternative. If nothing else, it will enhance your skill set to market an idea and then execute it.

## A success story

Even if you don't work for a large company, consider becoming an intrapreneur.

When I was running my IT services company, I always appreciated my employees bringing forward innovative ideas and solutions. Some of these ideas streamlined our services and added real profits back into the company.

As such, I always knew who the top performers were in my company, and in return I would give those individuals an extra bonus or raise.

In fact, our first employee started out as an unpaid summer intern. He was super hardworking and dedicated to adding value to our team. After he graduated, and with our business growing, we called him back to work for us as an entry-level support engineer. He did far more than his regular position and helped us to build new processes. He was awarded promotions quickly and eventually became a minority owner of the company.

You never know how your intrapreneur efforts will be rewarded.

# INTRAPRENEURSHIP WORKSHEET

It's quite common for full-time employees to have some extra time throughout the week. How many hours do you have to yourself each week?

What additional talents and values could you bring to your employer outside of your normal job description?

Does your company offer project-based bonuses? Have you ever asked?

Brainstorm 10+ ideas for a side project that could benefit you and your employer. It should be a win-win for both sides. Maybe you're getting experience by taking on a new project, or there's a related bonus upon completion.

Would becoming an intrapreneur help you build confidence toward becoming an entrepreneur, or at least starting a side hustle at home?

# GETTING PAID WHAT YOU'RE WORTH

**ARE YOU GETTING PAID EXACTLY WHAT YOU BELIEVE YOU'RE WORTH? NOT ENOUGH? LET'S CHANGE THAT.**

Let's say that you don't work for a company with great intrapreneurship opportunities, but you do earn a decent salary. Let's also assume that the company policy is rigid and allows only up to a 6% raise annually with a 10% bonus potential. That sounds pretty restrictive, with limited upward mobility career-wise.

Yet despite what the company policy states, there's almost always flexibility within a company to pay people more. And sometimes it can be a lot more.

Part of accessing more money within your company is adding value, and knowing your own market value. This means keeping an eye on salary ranges and rates for the specific type of work you're doing. There are websites like glassdoor.com that let you see what other companies are paying, as well as the employees' overall satisfaction ratings.

If you already know that you're providing great value to your company, don't feel bad about asking for a raise. You can do this at any time; you don't need to wait for your annual review. Come prepared, however, with why you should earn more, and the data to back it up. Also, if you want more leverage, consider job vacancies elsewhere.

My brother-in-law worked for a major corporation in their executive legal department. While he enjoyed his work, he was constantly keeping an eye out for other opportunities. And when he found them, he was able to negotiate a substantial raise with his current company. Remember, it's much more costly for a company to find a new "great" employee than it is to pay you more.

If you do choose this strategy, negotiate fairly and do your best to remove your emotions. Try to consider your employer's perspective and you'll be in a much better position to get what you want.

Negotiating doesn't always need to be about money. Does your company have training opportunities? One of my friends had his entire MBA paid for by his employer—a significant investment in his personal development. And if your company won't pay for all of it, a subsidy for half could still be worthwhile. Remember, once you're done, you retain that knowledge and become even more valuable to your company.

Don't forget, your mind is your biggest asset. No company or job can ever own that. Value yourself highly and others will too.

To achieve FIRE it's much easier if you can tap into new sources of income and growth. There are opportunities everywhere, even at your current job. You just need to look around.

# GETTING PAID WHAT YOU'RE WORTH WORKSHEET

How much do you currently get paid at your existing job? (If you're self-employed, you should answer this too.)

_____

What is the market (current) rate of pay for someone who does your type of work? (If you don't know, it's time to research it.)

_____

Typically there will be a range of rates of pay. What do you need to do to reach the top 10% of this range? If you're already there, is there an opportunity to grow into a new position that has a higher-end range?

_____
_____
_____

When was the last time you asked for a raise? Was it justified? If you didn't, what stopped you?

_____
_____
_____

How can you add more value to your company?

_____
_____
_____
_____
_____
_____

Who do you admire in your company, and is there any way to work with or be mentored by them?

_____
_____
_____
_____

Does your company offer other benefits, like subsidized education?

_____
_____
_____

# MANAGING YOUR RISK WITH INSURANCE

**WHEN YOU'RE YOUNG AND HAVE FEW ASSETS TO PROTECT, YOU MAY NOT THINK TOO MUCH ABOUT PROTECTION AND INSURANCE.**

However, as you get older and begin building your FIRE assets, and even a family, you'll want to start having this conversation internally and/or with your family.

Insurance can be a phenomenal tool to protect your progress. There are many different types of insurance to offset the negative effects when "bad things" occur; you're likely already familiar with some, but there are probably others that you may not know about.

Taking on insurance is a bit of a balancing act, because there is risk involved with doing anything. Insurance is just a way to balance out your risk aversion (how much risk you're willing to take) for a price.

The farther along your path to FIRE you are, the more you may begin to value this protection.

Suppose there are one hundred people in a health insurance group

→ With a 1% chance that any one of them could get sick and require $10,000

→ But no one knows who will get sick

If each person pays $100 into a "pool," that will collectively have $10,000 to cover the medical costs of the person who gets sick

→ So everyone gives up $100, but nobody loses more than $100

→ Ninety-nine people don't collect anything, but they do gain peace of mind and protection against a large loss

**Insurance shifts the risk of big loss from the individual to the insurance company**

## Different types of insurance

- Health/Medical Insurance
- Dental Insurance
- Renters Insurance
- Homeowner's Insurance
- Business E&O Insurance
- Property Insurance
- Travel Insurance
- Life Insurance
- Workers' Compensation Insurance
- Title Insurance
- Car Insurance
- Pet Insurance
- Product Insurance (Extended Warranties)
- Umbrella Insurance

As you can see, there's no shortage of insurance products! You'll need to decide which protections are worth it for your particular situation; your insurance needs while you're working to achieve FIRE will likely be different from those for your retirement.

Many young families begin looking at term life insurance as a failsafe for their family, while if you're a business owner or landlord, you'll want to protect your assets and limit your exposure to personal liability. Good insurance can help.

## Insurance after retiring early

As you continue to build out your FIRE plan, the insurance that is most often of concern in early retirement is health/medical insurance.

You want to have a reasonable assurance that your health will be taken care of if any major complications befall you while retired. Yet health insurance can be a significant cash flow variable to consider when planning your projections.

## Health insurance ideas for early retirement:

✓ Get coverage through government-sponsored or subsidized programs (e.g., ACA—Affordable Care Act)

✓ Get health care internationally—remember Jim, who moved to Panama? He has access to health care at cheaper rates than in the US

✓ Consider BaristaFIRE, in which you work a minimum number of hours part-time or just enough to be able to participate in an employer-sponsored plan

✓ Consider starting your own business after early retirement and take advantage of small business health insurance plans

✓ Need temporary insurance? If you're considering higher education in retirement, you may be able to access student health insurance

**GETTING** *started*

**START WITH THE**
*end in mind*

*Outline your*
**FIRE**
**STRATEGY**

**MAP YOUR FIRE**
**MILESTONES**
*& celebration points*

*Taking massive* **ACTION**

**EVALUATING, ADJUSTING**
*& achieving results*

**ACHIEVE**
*the desired*
*outcome*

# 5

## Designing

### YOUR

# FIRE

**PLAN**

# GETTING *started*

**WE'VE COVERED ALL THE TOPICS BELOW SO FAR:**

✓ Why you should pursue FIRE

✓ How to identify and change your limiting money beliefs

✓ How to track your essential FIRE metrics: net worth and cash flow

✓ How to calculate your own FIRE number with the Rule of 25

✓ What the most effective FIRE saving and investing strategies are

✓ How to earn more and accelerate income

✓ Why now is the best time to start

Now it's time to put pen to paper and design your FIRE plan.

In this chapter, you'll unwrap your ideal FIRE vision and make it come alive with an interactive vision board. You'll also have the opportunity to identify your top values to ensure you work these into your vision as well.

Another part of the plan is getting very specific about the outcomes you want to achieve and identifying the strategies you intend to employ.

The plan also includes an outline for easy reference and a timeline of FIRE milestones to track your progress and celebrate your wins along the way.

Write in this book as much as possible, and feel free to extend your plan to a binder. The better organized you are, the easier it will be to find relevant information when you need it.

Have fun making your FIRE plan!

> **"A CLEAR VISION, BACKED BY DEFINITE PLANS, GIVES YOU A TREMENDOUS FEELING OF CONFIDENCE AND PERSONAL POWER."**
> **Brian Tracy**

**"VISION WITHOUT ACTION IS JUST A DREAM. A LOT OF ACTION WITHOUT A VISION IS JUST A PASSING OF TIME. BUT A VISION WITH ACTION CAN CHANGE THE WORLD."**

**MARLON SMITH**
(Motivational speaker,
Success By Choice)

# START WITH THE
## *end in mind*

## YOUR FIRE VISION BOARD

DESIGNING YOUR FIRE PLAN IS A LOT OF FUN. DURING THIS PART OF THE PROCESS, YOU GET TO LET YOUR IMAGINATION RUN WILD AND BEGIN MAPPING OUT ALL THE POSSIBILITIES THAT ACHIEVING FIRE WILL BRING. IT'S TIME TO TAP INTO YOUR VISION!

You know how to choose empowering beliefs now. And you know that reaching FIRE is achievable with the proper mindset and strategies.

So let's create a tool that will remind you of your destination on a daily basis and fuel your journey in mind and spirit.

### FIRE Vision Board

A vision board, or dream board, is a simple and powerful visualization tool: it could be a colorful collage of pictures, words, and ideas expressed as an image of your future.

A FIRE vision board is specific to your goal of achieving FIRE. You'll use this to illustrate the future you wish to create. Don't worry, you don't need to be a professional artist to design one, and it doesn't need to be perfect. It just needs to speak to you.

Although this project will be fun, you're doing it for a scientific reason as well. You're creating a visual anchor to your goal, which will train your brain's focus and bring your subconscious thoughts in line with this outcome. It will also strengthen and enhance your emotions about FIRE.

### Creating your FIRE Vision Board

**Suggested materials**

- Poster board or cardboard
- Colored paper
- Corkboard
- Index cards
- Colored pens
- Paint
- Glue or glue gun
- Stapler, clips, or pins
- Ruler
- Scissors
- Magazines, ads, and photos

## Creating an empowering FIRE Vision Board

Need some visual inspiration? You'll find thousands of ideas for vision boards on Pinterest, or by searching online.

Don't forget to have fun with this. The goal is to get something completed that you can look at now. So give yourself a time limit and don't leave it unfinished. You can always add to it or modify it later.

1. Read through the vision board worksheet (see page 140)

2. Complete the value exercise (see pages 142–44)

3. Find pictures, words, and colors that represent how life will be for you after achieving FIRE

4. Write or cut out words that motivate you and remind you of your values

5. Create a collage that speaks to your FIRE vision

6. Hang it somewhere you can see it every day

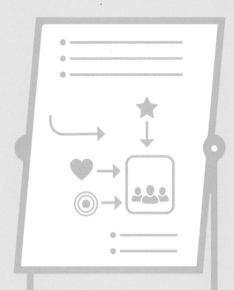

# FIRE VISION BOARD WORKSHEET

Use this FIRE Vision Board Worksheet to draw out your vision of what your FIRE life will look like.

## My FIRE vision

**List all the ways that you will enjoy life outside of working. What fun and creative activities would you pursue?**

-------------------------------------

-------------------------------------

-------------------------------------

-------------------------------------

-------------------------------------

-------------------------------------

-------------------------------------

**With so much free time, what new opportunities would be available to you?**

-------------------------------------

-------------------------------------

-------------------------------------

-------------------------------------

-------------------------------------

-------------------------------------

**Who will you spend your time with?**

-------------------------------------

-------------------------------------

-------------------------------------

-------------------------------------

-------------------------------------

**What will happen to your relationships?**

-------------------------------------

-------------------------------------

-------------------------------------

-------------------------------------

-------------------------------------

-------------------------------------

**Who will you become when you can focus on yourself and others freely?**

-------------------------------------

-------------------------------------

-------------------------------------

-------------------------------------

-------------------------------------

-------------------------------------

# WHAT DO YOU VALUE MOST?

**DID YOU ENJOY THE VISION BOARD EXERCISE? IT WAS FUN, RIGHT? NOW IT'S TIME TO EXTEND THAT CLARITY WITH A VALUES EXERCISE.**

Chances are that the dreams you expressed in the last section will be related to the values you uncover here. It's important that they be aligned to give your FIRE plan the best opportunity to thrive.

## What are your values?

Values are the things that you feel are important to living. As such, they help you to prioritize what you should be focusing on in life.

As someone who's seeking FIRE, I'm going to guess that you value freedom. Those who seek freedom operate in a different way from those who value restraint.

Of course, you have more than one value, and that's part of what makes you unique. So let's identify what those values are, and then distill them into your top five core values.

The reason for this is that your FIRE plan should incorporate your values both pre-FIRE and post-FIRE. It's the space where you'll find the most fulfillment. If it's not written down, it's easier to lose focus.

*Did you know?*

You're most happy when you're moving toward a goal.

Not only does a goal provide excitement but as you make progress toward it, your brain releases dopamine (aka the "feel good" transmitter).

Furthermore, when your goals align with your values, taking action requires less effort. You feel pulled toward your goal, rather than pushing yourself to create something you don't really believe in.

Have a look at the words below and circle all that resonate with you, then use the worksheet on page 144 to analyze your choices. Don't overthink it.

| | | |
|---|---|---|
| Abundance | Collaboration | Fairness |
| Acceptance | Commitment | Family |
| Accountability | Community | Flexibility |
| Achievement | Compassion | Forgiveness |
| Advancement | Connection | Freedom |
| Adventure | Consistency | Friendships |
| Advocacy | Contribution | Fun |
| Ambition | Cooperation | Generosity |
| Appreciation | Courage | Grace |
| Attractiveness | Creativity | Growth |
| Autonomy | Credibility | Happiness |
| Balance | Curiosity | Health |
| Being the Best | Daring | Honesty |
| Benevolence | Decisiveness | Humility |
| Boldness | Dedication | Humor |
| Brilliance | Dependability | Impact |
| Calmness | Diversity | Inclusiveness |
| Caring | Empathy | Independence |
| Certainty | Encouragement | Individuality |
| Challenge | Enthusiasm | Innovation |
| Charity | Ethics | Inspiration |
| Cheerfulness | Excellence | Integrity |
| Cleverness | Expressiveness | Intelligence |

| | | |
|---|---|---|
| Intuition | Popularity | Simplicity |
| Joy | Power | Sincerity |
| Justice | Preparedness | Sophistication |
| Kindness | Proactiveness | Spirituality |
| Knowledge | Professionalism | Spontaneity |
| Leadership | Prosperity | Stability |
| Learning | Punctuality | Strength |
| Love | Quality | Success |
| Loyalty | Recognition | Teamwork |
| Luxury | Relationships | Thankfulness |
| Making a Difference | Reliability | Thoughtfulness |
| Mindfulness | Resilience | Tradition |
| Minimalism | Resourcefulness | Trustworthiness |
| Motivation | Responsibility | Understanding |
| Open-Mindedness | Responsiveness | Uniqueness |
| Optimism | Risk Taking | Usefulness |
| Originality | Safety | Versatility |
| Passion | Security | Vision |
| Peace | Self-Control | Warmth |
| Perfection | Selflessness | Wealth |
| Performance | Service | Well-Being |
| Personal Development | Significance | Wisdom |
| Playfulness | Silliness | Zeal |

Take a look at all the values you circled on the previous page. Is there any overlap? If so, separate them by writing them into five different groups.

E.g., you might group:

- Caring
- Compassion
- Kindness
- Thoughtfulness

These are all similar values. However, you feel like "compassion" is the word that resonates with you best. So you could circle it here and add it to the list below, along with your other "top" values.

**Top Value #1**

_____

**Top Value #2**

_____

**Top Value #3**

_____

**Top Value #4**

_____

**Top Value #5**

_____

**Feel free to go back to your vision board and add in some values.**

**What do you value most?**

_____
_____
_____
_____
_____

**Where do you find fulfillment?**

_____
_____
_____
_____
_____

**Who are your heroes?**

_____
_____
_____
_____

# KNOW YOUR SPECIFIC OUTCOME

**SO YOUR FIRE VISION IS IN PLACE AND YOU'VE IDENTIFIED YOUR CORE VALUES. NOW IT'S TIME TO GET SPECIFIC.**

## SMART Goals

A SMART Goal will help you to define an outcome, along with some additional parameters to make it effective.

**S** = Specific
**M** = Measurable
**A** = Attainable/Achievable
**R** = Related
**T** = Time Bound

I'd like to share with you my goal when I was in my early twenties: to have a net worth of $1,000,000 by age thirty, and to have the option to retire early.

Now bear in mind that FIRE wasn't a conventional term back then. All I knew was that $1,000,000 sounded like a fair amount of money, so that's what I set my sights on.

If I had a time machine to go back and do it again, here's what I would have written:

**Specific:** My goal was to have a net worth of $1,000,000 or more by age thirty, with a stream of passive income of $6,000 per month or more from both rental properties and stock dividends.

**Measurable:** Since I'd quantified the amounts, it would have been easy to track via monthly net worth and cash flow reports.

**Achievable:** This one would have been the hardest to know. However, I believed I could do it, so I forged ahead.

**Related:** Luckily, my path to FIRE aligned naturally with my goals. I was able to perform important work creating value for others, and I genuinely had fun with my business partners and employees.

**Time Bound:** Since I was tracking my progress, I knew pretty closely when my net worth goal was in reach. I hit this when I was twenty-nine and haven't looked back since.

What I didn't know about FIRE at the time is that net worth doesn't automatically create cash flow. It needs to be invested in a compoundable vehicle. And while I had more than half of my assets invested, I was also carrying a lot of dead equity. Dead equity is value you have stored in a property that doesn't provide a good return on investment. Luckily, my wife still wanted to work, so we had a cash flow buffer to make my BaristaFIRE transition easier.

What's fascinating is that I was able to reach my net worth goal without thinking about it every day. Instead, I set it and forgot about it for a while. It's amazing what your brain will do for you if you chart the course first. My guess is that had I gone into it in more detail (like you're going to), I would have managed to reach the passive income goal as well.

That's why you want to be as clear as possible about your vision, values, and outcome.

 **S** = Specific

 **M** = Measurable

 **A** = Attainable/Achievable

 **R** = Related

 **T** = Time Bound

# KNOW YOUR SPECIFIC OUTCOME WORKSHEET

## My FIRE outcomes

Be as specific as you can here and define SMART goals for yourself.

### 1. What is your FIRE number?

_____
_____
_____

### 2. How will you achieve your FIRE number? What actions and habits will you create to ensure that you're saving toward this goal?

_____
_____
_____
_____

### 3. What FI Accelerator are you going to focus on? Extreme savings/ Investing? Real estate investing? Entrepreneurship?

_____
_____
_____
_____

### 4. Where can you immediately cut expenses and create savings today?

_____
_____
_____
_____

### 5. What new income sources did you identify that you can pursue today?

_____
_____
_____
_____

### 6. When will you achieve FIRE? In how many years and months? How old will you be?

_____
_____
_____

# GETTING PROFESSIONAL HELP

**YOU ALONE SHOULD CARE ABOUT YOUR MONEY MORE THAN ANYONE ELSE. THIS MEANS THAT YOU SHOULD ULTIMATELY BE IN CHARGE OF IT AND TAKE FULL RESPONSIBILITY FOR IT.**

This requires you to take the time to understand the fundamentals, educating yourself in financial matters and creating a measurable FIRE plan. Once you have this in place, you can either self-manage the execution of the goal or consider some help along the way. There are a number of paid options to consider.

The challenge with paid options is figuring out *who* to pay for help. In the world of financial services, there are many sharks swimming in the waters, and you don't want to become a victim. Many times the lines between advice and sales become blurred, and if you're uneducated, it's much easier to be taken advantage of. In some cases, fees are hidden and very obscure.

You should also realize that financial professionals may not be familiar with FIRE. You may actually have to do some educating yourself and explain your FIRE plan. If the help doesn't align with your plan, it's time to move along quickly.

Yet despite the hidden traps, there are some excellent professionals out there who can assist you with reaching your goals consistently and effectively. To start, you'll want to know the term "fiduciary." This refers to the relationship of trust between you and another person or organization, in that they're acting in your best interest.

Now, you may be wondering why this word even needs to be clarified, because shouldn't all people who work for you act on your behalf? I used to make that assumption as well, yet it's not always true. Sometimes brokers working within the financial sector only need to provide you with "suitable" advice. That's tricky, because certain brokers could be selling you a product that gains them more in commission instead of actually offering you a product that best meets your needs. Remember, not all advisors or brokers are equal. In fact, it's possible for a broker to be registered as a fiduciary independently, but not for the company they work for.

Thankfully, in recent years there has been some progress, with a Fiduciary Rule that requires brokers to act as fiduciaries when it comes to retirement planning assets.

As a general rule, you should always ask someone if they have fiduciary duties 100% of the time. You will also have to use your gut instincts too. Don't be afraid to ask a lot of questions.

Furthermore, because you're educated, you'll be better equipped to spot products and services that aren't aligned with your FIRE plan.

Here are some paid professionals who could potentially help:

- **Accountant**—when you're starting your FIRE journey, your taxes should be pretty simple. However, as you gain additional assets or potentially venture off into owning real estate or running a business, it could be time to seek professional help from an accountant who can provide you with the best advice for your particular situation.

- **Attorney**—lawyers sometimes get a bad rap, but a good one on your team can be well worth the hefty fee if they're protecting your assets and minimizing your liability.

- **Certified Financial Planner** (CFP)—an industry-recognized expert in the area of financial planning, estate plans, taxes, insurance, and retirement plans.

- **Banker**—a banker can be a key player on your team when you need money or financing for a business or real estate.

# Outline your FIRE STRATEGY

THE NEXT PART OF YOUR FIRE PLAN IS OUTLINING YOUR STRATEGY.

This can be broken up into two parts:

1. Your Core FIRE Strategy
2. Your FIRE Acceleration Strategy

## WHAT IS YOUR CORE FIRE STRATEGY?

Your Core FIRE Strategy consists of the logistical building blocks of your FIRE plan.

**INCOME:** What is your primary source? What strategies will you use to maximize it over time?

_____

_____

_____

_____

**SAVINGS:** What is your minimum savings/investing percentage, or dollar amount, that you will *always* pay to yourself first?

_____

_____

_____

**INVESTING:** What is your investment strategy? Are you actively participating in your employer's

retirement plan? Are you investing in your own retirement plan (e.g., Roth IRA, Traditional IRA, 401k/403b, Backdoor Roth, etc.)?

_____

_____

_____

_____

**INVESTMENT STRATEGY:** Will you be a passive index fund investor? Or will you be more active? Have you created an investor policy to ensure that you aren't scared out of the markets when they inevitably take a downturn at times?

_____

_____

_____

_____

# WHAT IS YOUR FIRE ACCELERATION STRATEGY?

**YOUR CORE FIRE STRATEGY IS THE BASELINE FOR REACHING YOUR FIRE GOAL. IT SHOULD BE A SOLID FOUNDATION THAT CAN STAND ON ITS OWN.**

However, once you're in the habit of saving and investing automatically, you may find you have some extra time on your hands. So, to cut your time to FIRE even faster, let's outline your FIRE Acceleration Strategy. All you need is one great investment or business idea to really fast-track your time to FI.

You have now learned about three different strategies to accelerate your path to FI.

- Extreme Savings
- Real Estate Investing
- Entrepreneurship

**Which of these will you start with? Why?**

_____

_____

_____

_____

_____

**What benefits do you hope to capitalize on with this strategy?**

_____

_____

_____

_____

_____

**Identify three additional resources through which to learn more about your FI Accelerator. What are they (books, courses, coaching, etc.)?**

_____

_____

_____

_____

**When will you begin? Who will you share this with?**

_____

_____

_____

# MAP YOUR FIRE MILESTONES
## *& celebration points*

## FIRE MILESTONES: THE TIMELINE

**THE LAST STEP IN DEFINING YOUR FIRE PLAN IS TO DETERMINE THE MILESTONES ALONG YOUR PATH TO ACHIEVING FIRE.**

Because this is a marathon, milestones will help you to appreciate your journey and define mini-celebration points along the way. They will also allow you to keep track of your progress and ensure that you're continually taking action to meet the next milestone.

In the milestones example opposite, we're making the assumption that FIRE will be achieved at $1,250,000. Your actual FIRE number may be lower or higher based on your preferences.

*Remember, the numbers and labels here are examples. With inflation constantly eroding the value of money, the figures or amounts may need to be adjusted upward depending on when you read this or what country you live in. Simply update the milestones to numbers that make sense to you.*

**$0** — **Getting to Zero** This can be a huge accomplishment for many. A lot of people fall victim to the consumerist sirens, but that doesn't mean you're doomed to stay there. I've seen many stories of individuals who have clawed their way out of debt through sheer will and determination. And don't forget, getting to zero likely means you've already created some momentum to carry you forward.

**$15,000** — **Your First Emergency Fund (three to six months)** Great job. You've intentionally directed your cash flow and saved a comfortable emergency fund of three to six months' worth of living expenses. Never will you need to live paycheck to paycheck again if you keep these funds intact. Let's keep moving and start investing!

**$100,000** — **Your First $100K** Some say that reaching your first $100,000 is the hardest. You've come from zero and are diligently raising your net worth. Now things are beginning to get interesting. If you can reach six figures, surely you can reach seven figures. Pat yourself on the back and let's move forward.

**$500,000** — **Halfway to a Million** It's amazing what can happen with consistent action. Your saving and investing habits are well founded now, and arriving at half a million is a reassuring reminder that you're gaining momentum. Growth is about to pick up.

**$1,000,000** — **The Millionaires' Club** Congratulations! You've reached millionaire status! This is no accident. Your beliefs and actions have led you here, and you have more choices now than you've ever had before. This milestone feels great, because you know you're not far away from your FIRE goal.

**$1,250,000** — **You're on FIRE** Incredible! You've done it. It's time to celebrate big-time. You've achieved FI your way, and your reward is freedom. What you do with your time now is completely up to you.

**Multimillions and Beyond** Just because you reach FIRE doesn't mean you have to stop earning money. Some say that reaching your second million and beyond is much easier than the first. You've mastered money and now have the ability to teach others too.

# YOUR FIRE MILESTONES WORKSHEET

## Let's create your own custom FIRE Milestones Timeline.

- To get started, what is your FIRE number?

- Feel free to borrow any milestones from the example, customize them, or create your own.

- How many milestones would you like to have? In the example, you'll see that there are five milestones before reaching FIRE at milestone six, and there's a post-FIRE milestone because some of you will inevitably want to continue pushing forward once you attain your FIRE number.

## My FIRE Milestones Timeline

Name your milestones, and then describe their significance.

1. _____

   _____

   _____

   _____

   _____

2. _____

   _____

   _____

   _____

   _____

3. _____

   _____

   _____

   _____

   _____

4. _____

   _____

   _____

   _____

   _____

5. _____

   _____

   _____

   _____

   _____

6. _____

   _____

   _____

   _____

# Taking massive ACTION

**WE'VE SPENT A LOT OF TIME ON DEVELOPING BELIEFS, LEARNING EFFECTIVE FIRE STRATEGIES, AND PLANNING. NOW IS THE TIME FOR ACTION!**

Because you've taken the time to craft a FIRE mindset, taking action won't be a problem. You may feel excited or a little anxious, but certainly ready to take on the challenge ahead.

## "DREAM BIG, START SMALL, BUT MOST OF ALL, START."
**Simon Sinek**

### Where to begin
Now that you have your FIRE plan, where will you begin?

The good news is that you've already started—learning and planning is taking action. And chances are that you know more about where you're at financially than ever before. That's perfect.

Continue your momentum by finding some easy, low-hanging fruit in your FIRE plan and then getting to work.

If a lot of this is new to you, take care of the fundamentals first. Continue your financial education. Wipe out that consumer debt. And begin building the habit of saving/investing each month.

If you're farther along, consider focusing on increasing your income and saving more. Review your portfolio and figure out if it's in line with your FIRE goal.

### Building momentum
The great thing about action is that if you do it often enough, it becomes easier. Aligning yourself with this momentum is the foundation for creating habits.

Allow these habits to work for you, just as you're making your money work for you.

*Start* **NOW!**

## BELIEFS > ACTIONS > RESULTS

## Take action anyway

I wish I could tell you that taking well-prepared and focused action always turns into the result you desire. But, alas, you probably already know that isn't true.

The good news, though, is that you've put yourself in the best place to win. But when things go awry, don't get discouraged.

My first eight years of investing in the stock market were rather disappointing. My accounts barely grew and I got discouraged, but I kept investing every month anyway.

It wasn't that my strategy was bad, but I'd hit a short-term bear market known as the "lost decade."

The good news is that by staying the course, I was eventually able to participate in the longest bull run in stock market history. This evened out the returns, and it's performing well.

I can't begin to tell you how many successful people I've met over the years who told me that their success was due to their taking action in the face of fear.

You can be completely prepared, but you will inevitably encounter situations when it's scary to take action.

Take action anyway.

Our best rewards in life (even outside of FIRE) are on the other side of our fears.

# CASE STUDY
## Taking Massive Action

If there's one guy I can think of who has taken more massive action than anyone to achieve FI, it would have to be Dom from GenYFinanceGuy.com.

Dom is an incredible individual. He wasn't born into privilege. In fact, his early life circumstances were the opposite. Dom's parents were drug addicts, and his dad spent an entire decade in and out of prison for selling crystal meth. His family lived on welfare, and he got into a lot of trouble when he was a kid.

By anyone's reasonable prediction, Dom could easily have found his way into a bad crowd and fallen into a life of drugs and crime. But he never became a victim of his circumstances. He had other plans.

Luckily, Dom was sent to live with his grandparents. It was there that he decided it was up to him to make his mark in life. He graduated with honors from both high school and college. He went to work in a corporate finance job where he excelled due to his dedicated work ethic. During this time he decided to learn everything he could about finance and FIRE.

Dom set some aggressive goals and got busy. He switched up companies strategically over the next few years and eventually landed an executive position at just shy of thirty years of age. Dom had increased his base salary by three times in a short couple of years! And as an intrapreneur, Dom was able to participate in building equity with his company.

Dom also lived relatively frugally given that he was earning six figures. It's been incredible to watch his cash flow and net worth explode in a span of a few years. Now Dom has ventured out on his own as a full-time entrepreneur and is set to become a seven-figure business in his first year out. His ability to take massive action is fueled by this optimism and ambition. Dom believes "everything" is learnable.

Outside of his impressive career path, Dom takes time to write his blog. He shares openly with other hardworking individuals how to take massive action and reap the rewards that come with it. He's an inspiration to many, and a fine example of someone who won't settle for less than he can be.

Although Dom is a prime candidate for FIRE, given his momentum, he'll likely ride FI for a while and keep building his empire into FatFIRE. He lives in Southern California with his wife and son, and, despite running a company, schedules a lot of family time.

> **"MONEY AND THE OPPORTUNITIES TO EARN IT ARE LIMITED ONLY BY YOUR OWN SELF-LIMITING BELIEFS."**
> **Dom (GenYFinanceGuy.com)**

# EVALUATING, ADJUSTING
## & achieving results

**AWESOME JOB! NOW THAT YOU'VE TAKEN MASSIVE ACTION, YOU WILL INEVITABLY GET RESULTS.**

And this is fantastic, because you're able to determine whether your strategies and associated actions are working.

If you've planned appropriately and have been modeling successful people, the chances are good that your results are positive.

The next question to ask is to what *degree* are the results positive? How effective are your actions? Is there an opportunity for improvement?

Let's take an example.

After reading *The FIRE Planner* you're inspired to spend more intentionally. You've cut out extraneous subscription services, you eat out less, and have even moved to an area of lower-cost housing. After all the cuts, you determine that you're saving an additional $1,000 per month.

You ask yourself, "What now?" Making the cuts seemed like a challenge in the beginning, but after living like this for a few months, you've formed a new baseline of comfort. "This isn't so bad. I don't feel like I'm missing anything, and I'm saving more money than ever before. Maybe I could find more areas to cut. And perhaps I could even find new areas to spend that are important to me."

Over the next couple of months, you reduce car consumption and use the saved gas money to purchase a nice used bike to transport yourself around. You're now saving $1,200 per month. Not only are you getting to places more efficiently but you're also finding a hidden health benefit as well. Keeping your heart rate up makes you feel more energized, and you feel happier and more focused.

Do you see in this example how you begin to analyze your results and then create momentum? It reinforces your empowering beliefs, which leads to new actions and then new results.

Stacking success is a remarkable thing, and it will become a habit if practiced often enough. And with enough adjustments and continued massive action, you will inevitably produce the results you desire.

You're doing an excellent job at being persistent if you've gotten this far.

## BELIEFS > ACTIONS > RESULTS

# MAKING ADJUSTMENTS WORKSHEET

Consider the new actions you're taking and answer the following questions for each one.

**1. What new action have you started and for how long?**

_____

_____

_____

**2. Are your results producing the desired outcome? Are they faster or slower than anticipated?**

_____

_____

_____

**3. How could your actions be adjusted to make your results better or more efficient?**

_____

_____

_____

**4. Were there any unintended side effects to this action?**

_____

_____

_____

_____

**5. What have you learned by taking this new action?**

_____

_____

_____

**6. Should you continue taking this action? If not, what action will replace it?**

_____

_____

_____

# ACHIEVE *the desired outcome*

ONCE YOU'RE CONSISTENTLY PRODUCING POSITIVE RESULTS, IT'S TIME TO LOCK IN THESE ACTIONS AS HABITS. THIS IS WHERE STACKING SUCCESS ON TOP OF SUCCESS WILL ULTIMATELY LEAD YOU TO YOUR LONG-TERM GOAL AND THE ACHIEVEMENT YOU DESIRE.

Furthermore, producing positive results reinforces the reason why you're taking action, and it will also solidify your empowered belief in what's possible.

Isn't it true that once you've achieved something, it's much easier to reproduce it the second time around? Isn't it also true that achieving a desired result gives you more confidence to move out of your comfort zone and try something

new? This could be in personal finance, or perhaps in a completely separate area (e.g., health and vitality).

This success formula can and will serve you in all areas of your life. The only thing left to do is to "rinse and repeat." Yes, keep doing it!

While it would be nice to program yourself like a machine, however, don't assume that it will be easy forever. Markets shift, and other

## Rinse and Repeat

Let's take a look back at where you've come from:

1.  You've shifted your limiting beliefs into empowering ones through inspiration and courage

2.  You've educated yourself about different vehicles to wealth and how they can apply to FI

3.  You've created a FIRE plan that will lead you to ultimate freedom

4.  You've begun to execute the plan with massive amounts of action

5.  You've seen the results, evaluated them, and adjusted your actions to achieve your desired outcome

variables change, so you'll need to be flexible and constantly check back within the evaluation stage.

Life and FIRE are nonlinear journeys, so don't get dismayed if you slip up, falter, or lose momentum. The important part is to remember that you were able to achieve once before, and you can do it again.

## Finding fulfillment and joy

It can be incredibly fun to create wins along the journey to FIRE— just remember to celebrate the little wins as well as the big ones! It's even possible to celebrate the mistakes and setbacks too. Remember, you have the ultimate power of perspective.

Ask yourself an empowering question like, "What else could this mean? What's something new I learned from this setback?" You can never really fail if you learn something from it. Part of achievement is exploring, falling down, getting back up, and learning to run forward.

## Keep your eyes on the prize

Because achieving FIRE is a marathon more than a sprint, it's important to keep your focus on the "prize." Review your FIRE plan often and remember to integrate your personal vision board (see page 138) into your daily life.

The amazing thing about achieving FIRE is that the second half feels much faster than the first. Once you begin to accelerate your earnings, increase your savings, and have compound interest work for you, you'll have a lot of positive momentum to push you past the finish line.

# YOUR FIRE PLAN SUMMARY: BRINGING IT ALL TOGETHER

All right, you've done a lot of work and played full out, and you now have a detailed plan to help you achieve FIRE.

However, it's also wonderful to have a simplified plan that you can reference quickly that's both clear and concise.

The more complex a plan is, the harder it is to follow. So take the time now to consolidate your FIRE plan into an easy-to-read FIRE Plan Summary.

## My FIRE Plan Summary

**1. Focus on the FIRE Vision Board you've created. Write down your FIRE vision in words:**

_____

_____

_____

_____

_____

_____

**2. What are your core values?**

_____

_____

_____

_____

_____

**3. Specific outcome—What are the SMART FIRE goals you've established for yourself?**

_____

_____

_____

_____

_____

_____

Between your FIRE Vision Board and this FIRE Plan Summary, you should have an incredible foundation to launch from.

Now all you need to execute your plan is a little determination, a lot of persistence, and the ability to be flexible. Believe that you can and you will.

# "A CLEAR VISION, BACKED BY DEFINITE PLANS, GIVES YOU A TREMENDOUS FEELING OF CONFIDENCE AND PERSONAL POWER."

**BRIAN TRACY**

*Celebrate!*

**RETIRING EARLY**

*Post* **FIRE**

6

**YOU'RE ON**

F I R E

*—Now What?*

# Celebrate!

## CELEBRATION: REFLECT AND REVIEW

**WOW. CONGRATULATIONS ARE CERTAINLY IN ORDER! YOU'VE DONE A FANTASTIC JOB OF REACHING FI.**

What an incredible milestone. No doubt you've had to persist and grow as an individual to achieve this phenomenal feat. Now, don't forget to celebrate!

Sometimes you find yourself so focused on a goal that when you finally do reach it, you forget to notice the huge win in the moment. This is a reminder to live in the present and enjoy your accomplishment and the rewards that come with it.

Part of celebrating this journey to FI is reflecting on what you've learned along the way. Not only will this allow you to savor the moment but it will also give you additional perspective and insight.

As you pause and reflect, you will likely feel grateful and a sense of abundance. This is the feeling that you've worked so hard to find!

### Create a FIRE bucket list

Why not make a FIRE bucket list of all the awesome things you'll do in your new FIRE life. Not sure where to start? I'll share a few of my own ideas as an example.

- Go on a road trip with my family
- Learn a new language
- Play more piano
- Start a blog
- Go fishing in San Diego
- Volunteer at church
- Organize my garage
- Go to the beach
- Learn how to be the best dad ever

**What did you learn on your path to FIRE?**

_____

_____

_____

_____

**What's the best thing about achieving FIRE?**

_____

_____

_____

_____

**Who have you met because of this FIRE journey?**

_____

_____

_____

_____

_____

_____

**Who have you become during this journey?**

_____

_____

_____

_____

**How have you changed?**

_____

_____

_____

_____

### Review your FIRE Vision Board

What a perfect time to go back and review your FIRE Vision Board.

Has it been with you throughout your FIRE journey, or has it lived in your subconscious only?

Either way, now that you're here, you have the freedom to start checking off things you want to do when you're on FIRE. This is going to be fun!

At this point, you may consider converting your vision board items into a FIRE bucket list. This is a list of all the fun, engaging, and fulfilling activities you want to do in FI and/or early retirement.

# RETIRING EARLY

**YOU'VE SPENT A LOT OF TIME FOCUSING ON THE FI PART OF THE EQUATION. NOW IT'S TIME TO SPEND SOME TIME WITH THE RE (RETIRE EARLY) ELEMENT.**

## What is RE?

Retire early, or early retirement, is a point in time when you decide to no longer work for money prior to a traditionally accepted retirement age of around sixty-five.

RE completes the second half of the FIRE equation. However, RE is different to a traditional retirement for several reasons.

To start, let's have a look at the word "retirement." Dictionary.com defines this as: "the act of retiring or of leaving one's job, career, or occupation permanently, usually because of age." And most people think of a traditional retirement as a complete cessation of work.

RE is a bit different, because often early retirees have more than half of their expected life ahead of them, which presents some unique challenges and opportunities.

The largest challenge that early retirees must overcome initially is to determine an investment vehicle that can produce income for many decades into the future. As you now know, there are three primary wealth vehicles that can achieve these results—extreme savings/investing, real estate investing, or entrepreneurship. All of these can create passive streams of income that can cover your annual expenses to varying degrees, and ideally indefinitely.

The biggest opportunity that early retirees get is the reclamation of life's most precious asset: time. This time affords them the freedom to pursue any passion they so desire. They're free to work, or not work. People often question whether an early retiree is truly "retired" if they've gone on to build a business or pursue some enterprise in their spare time. But, yes, they are still considered an early retiree.

Early retirees are defined by their freedom to choose any path. It may not fit tightly into the definition of "traditional retirement," but that's okay. RE is all about choice. And working can actually be a wonderful thing if you're focused on a passion that's in line with your values.

---

### ☀ FIRE TIP

Early retirees who work are not actually retired—true or false?

This is false. Early retirees are not defined by work or by income but rather by their ability to choose exactly what they want to do with their time without monetary limitations.

---

# ARE YOU READY?

## TO RETIRE OR NOT TO RETIRE—THAT IS THE QUESTION!

You've worked hard to earn FI. But are you ready to retire early? If so, let's go. If not, that's okay too.

It's time to let you in on a little secret: FIRE doesn't just have to mean Financial Independence, Retire Early. It could also mean **Financial Independence, Retire Eligible**, which I believe is a bit more accurate.

This simply means you've found freedom through FI, and you're ready to retire early at any time you choose. Your persistence and diligent action have created that freedom, and no one can take it away from you. How does this acronym make you feel?

### RE options
Before we go any farther, let's acknowledge the RE options you have available:

1. Stop working completely
2. Remain working and add to your FIRE nest egg
3. Cut back your hours significantly and work part-time
4. Quit your current job and take on new work within an area of true passion

As you can see, you have more choices available to you than just "retire" or "not retire." In fact, you can customize any variation of these choices to suit you.

Use the resources on pages 170–71 to help you to determine if you're ready or not.

### Don't retire early
If you choose not to retire early, there's not too much to do other than keep working. What made you choose this option? Do you still plan to retire early, but just a little farther out? Revisit your FIRE plan and adjust it accordingly.

### Part-time work
If you choose a part-time schedule, you'll want to discuss this option with your employer. There may be certain hourly requirements in order to be eligible for specific benefits such as health care coverage.

This is a hybrid model in which you can still grow your nest egg, and at the same time have a lot of additional free time to yourself.

What other plans or projects will you take on in your spare time? Go back and adjust your FIRE plan to match your new goals.

### Retire early
So you decided to follow your FIRE plan as it was laid out. What's going to be the best thing about retiring early?

As you consider this, make a Retire Early Plan in further detail. You'll want to revisit where your retirement income will come from, health care coverage, and worst-case scenario planning. Working through these ideas up front will give you the confidence to move into early retirement with ease.

## Reasons to Retire Early

- To live a simpler lifestyle
- The freedom to travel/explore without required hours of work
- You have 25 times or more living expenses
- You're ready for the next chapter of life
- You want to spend more time with loved ones
- 
- 
- 
- 
- 
- 
- 
- 
- 
- 
- 
- 
- 
- 
- 

## Reasons to Keep Working

- You can keep building your FIRE nest egg
- You enjoy the work you do
- You enjoy the people you work with
- The work is fulfilling
- Your work is part of your identity and makes you proud
- 
- 
- 
- 
- 
- 
- 
- 
- 
- 
- 
- 
- 
-

# RETIRING EARLY WORKSHEET

Are you ready for early retirement? This worksheet will help you decide.

**What are you most excited about with early retirement?**

_____

_____

_____

_____

**What are your greatest concerns about early retirement?**

_____

_____

_____

_____

**Are you satisfied that your nest egg is large enough for you to quit your career?**

_____

_____

_____

_____

**Do you have a strategy to withdraw the funds needed to survive?**

_____

_____

_____

_____

_____

**Do you have supplemental cash flow from investments?**

_____

_____

_____

_____

**Are you ready to give up your career at your current company?**

_____

_____

_____

_____

# EARLY RETIREMENT WITHDRAWAL STRATEGIES

**OKAY, YOU'RE SATISFIED WITH YOUR FIRE NEST EGG AND YOU'VE DECIDED TO RETIRE EARLY. NOW YOU NEED TO DETERMINE THE BEST WAY TO WITHDRAW YOUR MONEY.**

Because you're retiring early, most of your traditional retirement accounts aren't accessible yet because you don't meet the minimum age to withdraw funds without paying an early withdrawal penalty.

For example, if you try to access funds directly from IRAs, 401ks, or other similar US investment accounts prior to age 59.5, you'll need to pay an early withdrawal fee of 10% on top of having to pay taxes on the distribution. This isn't an attractive withdrawal strategy given the amount of money that would vanish up front.

So bloggers like the Mad Fientist asked a better question: How can you access the money in your FIRE nest egg without triggering a penalty and/or unnecessary taxes?

Here are a couple of popular methods for accomplishing this:

## Roth Conversion Ladder

The first early withdrawal method is called a Roth Conversion Ladder. This does require a little pre-planning, but the benefits are definitely well worth the time spent.

You'll likely be contributing to a pre-tax IRA (e.g., 401k, 403b, etc.) during your earning years. Once you quit, you can move this over to a traditional IRA. Next, you'll convert a portion of your traditional IRA over to a Roth IRA. (This is a taxable event, so plan accordingly.)

Once the proceeds are in the Roth IRA, you'll need to wait five years to touch the money. But once it's "seasoned," you're free to withdraw the funds tax-free, and free from the 10% early withdrawal penalty.

**contribute** to pre-tax retirement accounts during your career to reduce your taxes

**retire** early!

**convert** from your traditional IRA to your Roth IRA

**transfer** your employer's retirement accounts to your traditional IRA

**wait** five years before touching the converted money

**withdraw** the conversion tax- and penalty-free!

As you continue doing conversions during early retirement, your taxes should be lower, as you're no longer earning income at the rate you once were. These are the "rungs" of your Roth Conversion Ladder.

This may sound very technical at first, but take the time to understand it. If you do plan on RE, this is an excellent method to move funds out penalty-free.

*Always check with a qualified tax professional before executing any plans. Rules and government regulations are constantly changing.*

*Some of these ideas are country-specific. Check your country's regulations to help plan and give yourself the best chance of minimizing your taxes and penalties.*

## Alternate Method—Rule 72(t)

Rule 72(t) allows individuals to withdraw funds from tax-deferred IRA accounts (e.g., 401k or 403b) early (before age 59.5) penalty-free, as long as SEPP requirements are met.

### SEPP = Substantially Equal Periodic Payments

You'll still be required to pay taxes on the proceeds, but you won't be subject to the 10% early withdrawal penalty. You'll need to calculate the requirements based on taking at least five SEPPs over the span of five years, or until you reach 59.5 years old. The amount of the payments needs to be calculated based on your life expectancy within approved IRS methods (amortization, life expectancy, or annuitization).

This rule is a bit more complex than the Roth IRA Conversion Ladder, but I want you to be aware that there are other possibilities in case one doesn't work out.

**contribute** to pre-tax retirement accounts during your career to reduce your taxes

**retire** early!

**determine** which SEPP calculation method is best for your scenario

**transfer** your employer's retirement accounts to your traditional IRA

**withdraw** the correctly calculated amount each year, penalty-free

**continue** the withdrawals for five years or until you turn 59.5, whichever is longer

# FAILSAFE—SEQUENCE OF RETURNS

**HAVE YOU DONE EVERYTHING ACCORDING TO YOUR FIRE PLAN? DID IT GO EXACTLY AS YOU ENVISIONED IT? IT'S UNLIKELY. NO MATTER HOW MUCH WE PLAN, WE WILL ALWAYS ENCOUNTER THE UNEXPECTED. THE FANTASTIC THING IS THAT YOU WERE ABLE TO ADAPT. AND REMEMBER THIS IDEA FOR POST-FIRE TOO.**

Just because you've achieved FIRE doesn't mean you can suddenly ignore your numbers. I'm sure you won't, given how much momentum you've built up over the past years. However, because the economy and the markets move in ways we can't always plan for, you'll need to be flexible.

For example, if you get lucky like I did and retire early into a long bull market, your chances of long-term retirement are fantastic. But what happens if you retire early into a bear market and you're withdrawing funds from your portfolio while it's shrinking in value? This concept is known as the sequence of return risk. In other words, your account withdrawals are more costly during a bear market than they are during a bull market.

While statistics are still on your side that you can weather a bear market, it may be daunting nonetheless. So, it's always good to build in a failsafe, or backup plan, in early retirement.

Remember the 4% Rule (see page 66) that you based your FIRE number on? Well, no one is going to stop you from pulling out a little less if you're going into a bear market. In some ways it may be prudent. And, you may find that withdrawing just 3% is doable until the markets return to positive territory.

Finally, don't forget that you can always go back to work if you so choose. Maybe you feel a little unsure about a particular time period we're living in, and you want to have an income supplement. There's no harm in exploring BaristaFIRE, in which part-time work can provide supplemental income, as well as the potential to access health insurance.

Remember, this is your FIRE story, and you can choose whatever works for you.

Use the following worksheet to plan your RE failsafe.

# FAILSAFE—SEQUENCE OF RETURNS WORKSHEET

You've spent a lot of time planning for nearly every scenario. However, what's your plan if you retire early into a bear market?

Use this worksheet to plan ways to navigate this uncertainty.

**1. Could you live on a lower annual budget? If so, how much less?**

**2. What are some additional ways you can supplement your income during early retirement?**

**3. Are you willing to return to work after ___ years if your FIRE nest egg drops to ___?**

**4. What other ways can you reduce your major expenses? For example, would you be willing to live in an RV to cut costs?**

**5. Have you rebalanced your asset allocation to mitigate market risks?**

**6. If you're retiring early into a bear market, have you considered working until the markets move back into bull territory? Or have you considered part-time work?**

# EXITING YOUR JOB

**YOU TAKE A DEEP BREATH AND MARCH CONFIDENTLY INTO YOUR BOSS'S OFFICE. THEY LOOK YOU SQUARE IN THE EYE AND SAY "WHY AREN'T YOU WORKING? DON'T TELL ME I NEED TO HELP YOU AGAIN. WILL YOU EVER GET YOUR JOB RIGHT?"**

You look back at them and grin.

"What's so funny? You'd better wipe that smug smile off your face, or you're going to regret it," they snap.

"I just came in here to tell you... I *quit*!" you exclaim, and promptly slam the door behind you.

Never again will you need to work for them. Little did they realize that you've been working on a FIRE plan all along. And that plan has just been executed with precision by you. You're officially retired!

Okay, so maybe this example doesn't quite mirror real life. Regardless, if you've been on the road to FIRE, then you've likely imagined your last day of work many times over.

Well, that time is finally here. You've decided to officially quit your job. But wait! Before you slam any doors, let's explore the most optimal way to do this.

First of all, make sure you've completed your Retire Early Worksheet. Does everything look good?

Okay, before you go in and hand over your resignation, ask your boss if there are any options that could benefit them on your way out.

Although the dramatic example above is exciting, in real life you'll want to avoid burning any bridges on your way out—even if you do have a pain-in-the-a$$ boss.

The reasons why you want to leave on good terms are:

- to have a good reference in the future (you never know what the future holds)

- your old company may be a future client if you decide to do some consulting work for them

- it's the nice thing to do, and leaving abruptly hurts your coworkers too

- they may give you the opportunity to be laid off instead of your needing to resign.

Speak with your HR (human resources) department before you leave. See if there are any options you need to be aware of prior to your departure. For example, they may have specific contact information for someone who could help you move your 401k into a rollover IRA.

Once you give official notice, it's important to treat people with dignity and respect on your way out. Realize that some coworkers may be jealous, so don't take any snide remarks personally. And make sure to turn in all company equipment so you don't need to return later. Also, try to get personal contact information from your coworkers in the event that you wish to connect with them later.

On your final day, you could even bring in treats to celebrate!

# 𝒫𝑜𝑠𝑡 FIRE

## THE JOURNEY CONTINUES

**HAVE YOU EVER RUN A REALLY LONG RACE OR ACHIEVED A GIGANTIC GOAL? WHAT HAPPENED AT THE END? CHANCES ARE YOU FELT A BIG SHIFT OF ENERGY. THIS IS YOUR MOMENTUM CHANGING.**

When retiring early, you could literally be working sixty hours a week, and then suddenly move to zero hours.

I know from firsthand experience that this feeling can be a bit bizarre. I remember my first weeks home after retiring early—the days suddenly seemed so long, and I felt like a fish out of water for the first month.

The strange thing was that I had so much freedom that I didn't know what to do with myself some days.

Over time, though, you'll realize that your newfound freedom is a new opportunity in itself. You've reclaimed your most precious resource—time. And the way to find fulfillment going forward is to create new goals!

The journey continues post-FIRE because the world needs you to step into your greatness.

Now consider what would happen if you rode your current momentum from achieving FIRE and redirected that energy into a new set of goals.

What would happen is that you'd get a fabulous head start!

So, why not set yourself up for additional success coming off a huge win achieving FIRE?

In the next section, we'll cover some potential new goals you may want to consider.

Money, of course, is a key component of wealth, but it's not the only ingredient. You also need to take care of your health and vitality. After all, what good is money if you aren't healthy enough to spend it?

How about relationships? Is this an area you can improve with your newfound time post-FIRE? What good is money if you can't share it with your loved ones?

I'll let you in on a little secret. You're happiest when you're on a journey and growing. So don't stagnate post-FIRE. Ride this huge wave of momentum and supercharge your next level of life.

It's time to be excited all over again!

# FINDING BALANCE

**LIVING A FIRE LIFE IS WONDERFUL, AND THERE ARE PLENTY OF ADVANTAGES THAT COME ALONG WITH IT.**

However, achieving FIRE doesn't suddenly make life perfect. Life is still life. There will be good days, and there may be a few bad days too. The key to optimizing the good days is finding balance in your post-FIRE life.

In this next exercise, we're going to revisit those core life categories, and you'll be able to assess the quality of life that you're living in each respective area. There's always something you can work on, right?

For each area of life, give yourself a rating from 1 to 10, with 1 being "terrible" and 10 being "outstanding."

Finding balance and growth across multiple areas of life is part art and part skill. And the beauty of your post-FIRE life is that you have the freedom to concentrate on what matters most to you, and the ability to shift your focus to different areas as needed.

Achieving balance is a skill you'll want to become very familiar with. It's a way to appreciate the present moment, and simultaneously have the foresight to plan for the future with new goals and aspirations.

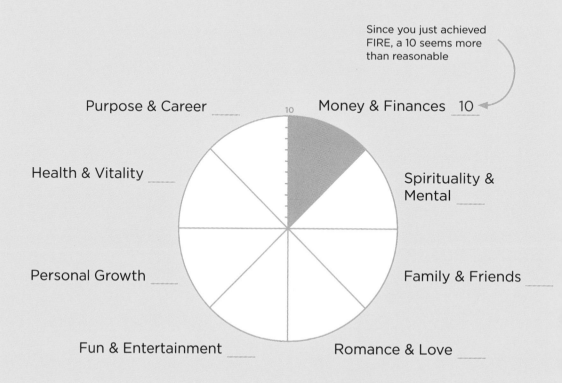

Since you just achieved FIRE, a 10 seems more than reasonable

Purpose & Career ____

Money & Finances  10

Health & Vitality ____

Spirituality & Mental ____

Personal Growth ____

Family & Friends ____

Fun & Entertainment ____

Romance & Love ____

# MAXIMIZING YOUR MOST VALUABLE ASSET: TIME

YOU ALREADY KNOW THAT TIME IS YOUR MOST VALUABLE ASSET. YOU'VE ACHIEVED FIRE! HOWEVER, IT'S WORTH NOTING AGAIN, ESPECIALLY POST-FIRE, THAT IT'S STILL IMPORTANT TO PROTECT AND VALUE YOUR TIME. YOU'VE DONE THE HARD WORK TO RECLAIM IT—NOW TREASURE AND ENJOY IT!

## Focus & attention

You may be asking yourself if this much planning is overkill. It's not.

Your focus and attention are constantly being bombarded by external sources. Planning allows you to prioritize what's important to you, not someone else.

## Protect your time & say "no"

The better an investor you become, the more often you'll begin to spot deals. Likewise, you may wind up on the mailing list of others trying to sell you on the next best deal or investment. This isn't a bad thing if the list sends opportunities your way, but you'll have to cut through clutter as well.

Others may see your success and want to ask you for advice, or perhaps your help, for free. You can certainly do this, but just be aware that time spent here is time lost elsewhere.

There are countless other ways that your time will be solicited. So become very familiar with the word "no." This is going to be your primary filter to block out the noise and concentrate on what's important to you.

## Planning for efficiency

Your schedule can be your best friend, but you've got to take some time to plan it out. It doesn't need to be done all at once, but consistency is the key. Consider planning your week in advance and ensuring that you have time scheduled for each new goal with a tangible action.

A scheduled day, week, month, or year is significantly more productive than an unscheduled one. Use technology to your advantage to become more efficient and ensure important activities aren't missed.

## Finding time to play

It's important to enjoy the financial freedom you've earned, so schedule some time to play.

What's your favorite pastime? Who do you enjoy hanging out with? Why not combine the two?

Consider planning a family trip or vacation months or even years in advance.

## Use timers & alarms

Scheduling your time with a smartphone can be efficient. However, with too many alarms constantly going off, it's hard to determine which ones you should be paying attention to.

To mitigate this barrage of notifications, consider using alarms and timers on your phone only for the most important tasks.

# WORKING FOR FULFILLMENT & FUN

**IT'S TEMPTING TO THINK THAT EARLY RETIREMENT IS ALL ABOUT LOUNGING AROUND AND NOT HAVING A CARE IN THE WORLD. HOWEVER, TIME AND TIME AGAIN, EARLY RETIREES COME BACK TO SOME FORM OF WORK, EVEN IF THEY DON'T NEED TO.**

The reason most early retirees return to work is that working when you don't need to feels very different from having to work.

What if you could simply work for fun and fulfillment? Now that you've achieved FIRE, you can do exactly that!

Consider that working post-FIRE can actually make you happy. In fact, more than ever, you'll be drawn to something in which you can create, grow, or give value.

Is there any type of career that you wish you'd gone into? Here's an opportunity to do just that, or simply explore for adventure. Imagine the possibilities now that you don't actually need to work:

- Teacher
- Coach
- Real Estate Agent
- Artist
- Entrepreneur
- Author
- Mentor
- Student of "X"
- Chef
- Contractor
- Consultant

Remember, you're no longer bound by money constraints, so you could also work for free as a volunteer, or you could earn some extra money. The choice is yours.

Here are a few famous people who continued to work even after retiring:

- ✓ Michael Jordan
- ✓ Magic Johnson
- ✓ George Foreman
- ✓ Michael Phelps
- ✓ Audrey Hepburn

## Bonus income

More often than not, early retirees are curious and eventually try out BaristaFIRE. This can not only be fun but also augment your existing FIRE nest egg and delay the need to touch any principal.

Just remember to consult with your tax professional to determine the tax ramifications of taking on additional income.

## Seasonal work

Don't want to work all year? Then consider seasonal jobs. These can be a fun way to earn additional income and interact with people, and give you a ton of flexibility with your time once the season is over.

This could be work related to increased demand during the winter, holiday season, or perhaps the warm travel months. I'm giving some close consideration to opening up a seasonal ice cream store that would keep me busy during the summer-time only.

## Have fun & think outside the box

Part of having fun is exercising your creativity.

What if you tried several new types of work? Variety appeals to a lot of people, so why not try a few different things? You can afford to.

Would it be fun to work with a close friend or family?

## Family & friends' time

One of the best gifts in post-FIRE is the freedom to spend more quality time with family and loved ones.

Although you may choose to work in some capacity, you will no longer be stressed about earning money. And without undue work stress, you'll find that your relationships have the potential to flourish.

With more time and freedom, you have the flexibility to meet loved ones during their most convenient times. Likewise, you'll have the luxury to be more intentional with others.

People don't necessarily remember what you tell them, but they will remember how you make them feel.

## Reach out

Have you lost touch with a handful of good friends over the years? Reach out. Chances are they're busier than you are now, but they'd be delighted to hear from you.

Enriching your life with strengthened relationships in post-FIRE shouldn't be missed. It's incredible.

## Mend old wounds

Have you had any relationships go sour over the years? Perhaps it was with a formerly close family member or friend. It's a funny thing, but in post-FIRE you begin to appreciate so much around you. So maybe it's time to heal old wounds. Does it really matter who's at fault any longer?

Forgiveness is another passage of freedom that you can open.

## Say what you mean

In post-FIRE you're getting to juice the finest fruits in life.

Be a light to others. Tell those you care about how much they mean to you.

Life is short. Make the most out of your relationships and you will always be rich.

## "MAKE YOUR VOCATION YOUR VACATION."
**Mark Twain**

### Gift your time

A thoughtful gift of time and presence can go much farther than any physical gift you can buy. It doesn't take a lot of money to create special experiences.

Here are some ideas that can help strengthen your relationships:

- Plan a family camping trip
- Organize a family reunion
- Plan a picnic date
- Make a movie montage for a birthday gift
- Read with your kids
- Play a video game with your kids
- Volunteer at a homeless shelter with your family
- Surprise your parents

The possibilities are endless!

But, as you already know, ideas are easy to come by. So take the time and extra effort to write down some that are important to you—and then make them real.

## WORKSHEET: STRENGTHENING RELATIONSHIPS IN POST-FIRE

| WHO | HOW/WHAT | WHEN |
|-----|----------|------|
|     |          |      |

Now, schedule these! Remember, you can always move times around later, so get something on the calendar now.

# LIVING HEALTHY

**POST-FIRE IS AN EXCELLENT TIME TO FOCUS ON YOUR HEALTH AND VITALITY. THE LAST THING YOU WANT TO DO IS EARN YOUR MONETARY FREEDOM ONLY TO BE SIDELINED BY A HEALTH ISSUE.**

You may not be able to prevent all disease and illness, but you can schedule the necessary time to focus on your well-being.

## Exercise

Keeping your heart active and increasing your stamina not only helps your longevity but also makes you feel happier. Exercise stimulates the secretion of chemicals in your body with positive benefits. Endorphins are released, which make you feel good and boost your mood. Furthermore, exercise can reduce your levels of stress, as it lowers your cortisol and adrenaline.

And since you'll be free when most other people are working, you have the added benefit of visiting workout facilities with little to no crowds.

## Eating well

In post-FIRE, you'll have time to eat more intentionally. You can prepare your own food and avoid "fast foods," which are notoriously unhealthy.

Take the time to learn about which types of food can support a healthy metabolism, and explore the benefits of eating a plant-based diet.

## Grow your own food

It's well documented that an organic diet provides health benefits over processed foods. Organically grown foods also contain fewer pesticides and are better for the environment.

However, eating organic foods is also associated with higher costs. The good news is you can mitigate these additional costs by growing your own food. This will save you from both higher costs and harmful chemicals.

If you choose to eat meat, you could even farm your own livestock.

## Activity & fun

Sometimes exercise or being intentional with your diet can seem cumbersome. But just like your FIRE journey, it requires discipline to reap the long-term rewards. For some positive momentum, figure out a way to have fun—perhaps by playing a favorite sport with friends or family. Do you like competition? Integrate that into your workout routine.

And when it comes to eating well, find accountability partners and break the old habits together.

## Meditation

Take time to quiet your mind. You are the master of your time and calendar now, so consider integrating some new positive habits, such as meditation, into your life. Meditation not only helps to center your thoughts but can also have further health benefits like decreasing blood pressure and improving sleep. Consider doing yoga if you want to combine the meditation components with some physical activity.

# CREATING A WEALTH LEGACY

YOU CAN DO A LOT OF GOOD WITH YOUR MONEY WHILE YOU'RE STILL ALIVE. AND THE GOOD NEWS IS THAT YOU CAN DO EVEN MORE POSITIVE THINGS WITH YOUR MONEY WHEN YOU FINALLY PASS AWAY. IN FACT, YOU CAN HAVE YOUR ASSETS DIRECTED EXACTLY AS YOU WISH USING INSTRUMENTS SUCH AS WILLS AND TRUSTS.

It's no secret that you can't take your money with you when you die, so creating your wealth legacy is an important step in the FIRE process. Ideally, you started this process before reaching FIRE. However, many choose to wait until later in life to think about these logistics.

What's important is that you address it now in relation to your FIRE life.

## Plan to outlive your money

Is it possible that you'll outlive your money? Anything can happen, but you've put conservative measures into place that will allow your FIRE nest egg to thrive throughout your entire retired life and even beyond.

Thus, there's a good chance that you'll have amassed a significant asset base that you can pass on to loved ones, friends, and charitable causes you're passionate about.

How do you want to be remembered at the end? Who would you like to help?

Remember that money is a tool, and not everyone will know how to use this tool. So, consider how and to whom you will pass along your wealth. Will your heirs be ready to assume the responsibility?

If you have money to give, what are the ramifications of doing so?

## Match intentions with thoughtful actions

Part of your legacy may be teaching others how to "fish" for themselves. Although it may be easier to hand over monetary gifts, sometimes, while well intended, it can inhibit people's natural drive to succeed.

My wife and I always planned to pay for our kids' education through college. However, we've had a change of heart lately. Sometimes you need to create an environment that taps into your survival instinct and allows growth. So, while we intend to supplement their educational costs, we also want them to have some ownership too, by paying for a portion of it.

## What will be your wealth legacy?

In post-FIRE, you have the advantage of time on your side. You can be highly thoughtful in your planning and cover the details in full.

Consider where your money will have the largest impact. Are there other people or organizations in your life that you want to help in your absence? Take the time to create a wealth legacy that aligns with your values and gives you a sense of maximum contribution.

# ESTATE PLANNING

**AN INCREDIBLE OPPORTUNITY WITH FIRE IS THE ABILITY TO CONTINUE TO GROW YOUR ASSETS EVEN DURING YOUR EARLY RETIREMENT. THIS COULD HAPPEN NATURALLY, IF YOU RETIRE INTO A BULL MARKET, OR YOU MAY CHOOSE TO HAVE SOME SIDE HUSTLES. EITHER WAY, THERE'S A DECENT POSSIBILITY THAT YOU'LL HAVE MORE ASSETS THAN YOU'LL NEED DURING YOUR LIFETIME.**

If you have a family, then chances are good that you may already have started an estate plan. If not, now is a great time to start, especially since you've already accumulated a healthy base of assets. This could be a considerable portion of your wealth legacy if you choose to pass it down through the generations.

Below are some important tools for passing along generational wealth.

## Designated beneficiaries

When signing up for an investment account, one of the questions asked is who your beneficiaries are. This is simply a way for you to name who gets the proceeds of your account in the event of your death. For example, you may choose to put your spouse, child, or other loved one. It could all go to one person, or it could be split across multiple heirs. You could also designate a trust if you so choose.

## Will

A will is a document that expresses your wishes as to how your property is distributed upon your death. This gives you the final say on where your assets go during probate. If you don't have a will, the distribution of your assets will be decided by the state courts in probate according to their process.

## Revocable trust

A revocable trust is a similar instrument to a will in that it can transfer assets to your heirs according to your instructions. It also has the added benefit of becoming active immediately upon creation, and it can help your heirs to avoid probate completely and keep your assets private even after your death. You may have both a will and a trust, as there are some specific things you can accomplish with each. For example, a will can specify guardianship for minors, while a trust cannot.

## Life insurance

Life insurance pays out a benefit upon your death to a designated beneficiary. You may consider this type of insurance to mitigate the risk of an untimely death for your family. Term life insurance is used as a way to hedge against tragedy for your family while you're still working. However, even in post-FIRE, life insurance can play a role in your overall estate plan.

*Speak with a qualified attorney and/or tax professional to structure your intentions in the best manner possible.*

# BEYOND MONEY

WITH THE MAJOR STRESS OF MONEY OUT OF THE WAY, IN YOUR POST-FIRE LIFE YOU CAN ENGAGE FREELY IN AREAS TYPICALLY NOT ASSOCIATED WITH GENEROUS COMPENSATION. I'VE PERSONALLY FOUND REFUGE IN SOME OF THESE CREATIVE OUTLETS AS A MEANS OF BALANCING OUT MY LIFE.

## Writing

There are numerous opportunities to write during your post-FIRE life. You can start your own blog and share your thoughts and ideas, or you could write as a freelancer for another blog. Your story of achieving FIRE could inspire others, and sharing your process is both cathartic and generous.

But don't limit yourself to writing online. Have you ever wanted to write a book? It could be completely unrelated to finances. Perhaps you have specialized knowledge in a particular area you want to share. Or maybe you've always wanted to bring a character to life in a novel. There's no better opportunity to write freely!

## Art

Art is subjective and a tough industry to make a living in. However, in your post-FIRE life you have the freedom to explore this to your heart's content. Try out different types of art: painting, sketching, 3D, sculpture, and even digital art. The possibilities are many, and you can find a whole array of instructional videos online for free.

How about acting or stand-up comedy? Here's your opportunity to explore interests that you may never have entertained. Not only will you improve your speaking ability but you can explore an entirely different side of yourself. You may not become the next Academy Award winner, but you'll build confidence nonetheless.

## Coaching & teaching

One of the most fulfilling activities is to become a coach or teacher. What special gifts do you have that you can teach to others? What comes easy to you that's hard for others?

Coaching and teaching not only share the best parts of you but it's amazing to watch someone's eyes light up. It's the very reason I wrote this book—to share the seed of FIRE knowledge that can change your life.

In the process of teaching others, you also begin to master the subject yourself. It's a win-win for all.

## Volunteering

There are many organizations and movements that need your energy. Without it, they can't survive, because it's not economically feasible. What calls to you? Are there places to volunteer that you've always wanted to be a part of?

Nowadays, volunteering could be in person or even online. Either way, you're helping to provide value to others and making an impact with your most precious resource—time.

# PAYING IT FORWARD

**REACHING FIRE IS AN INCREDIBLE ACCOMPLISHMENT AND GIFT. YOU ARE ONE OF THE FEW WHO'VE TRULY FOUND FREEDOM BEYOND A PAYCHECK. THIS IS ABUNDANCE AND WEALTH THAT MOST PEOPLE WILL ONLY EVER DREAM OF.**

Thank you for allowing me to be a small part of your journey. If you found just one great idea contained within this book, I'd like to ask you for a favor: Teach that idea to someone else.

How awesome would our world be today if everyone took the time to pay it forward?

I know for myself that I would never have reached this point in my life without the help and generosity of family, friends, and even strangers.

It takes only a few minutes to share the idea of FIRE with those who've never heard of it. Dare to light a new passion in others by living out your own FIRE dream with authenticity and humility.

Offer to help those who are less fortunate to find their footing. Encourage them to fight for the potential you know they possess. It's the same inner journey we're all faced with.

## The end is only the beginning

At the beginning of your FIRE journey, you may have thought there was no end in sight. And when you finally achieved it, you realized that this is only the beginning of additional growth and expansion.

The FIRE is spreading, and shining a new path for those bold enough to seek it. Do your part to cheer others on. The world needs your leadership, your passion, and your FIRE.

Thank you also for taking the time to invest in you. You are truly remarkable, and I look forward to hearing your own FIRE story from you someday soon.

> **"SUCCESS IS DOING WHAT YOU WANT TO DO, WHEN YOU WANT, WHERE YOU WANT, WITH WHOM YOU WANT, AS MUCH AS YOU WANT."**
> **Tony Robbins**

If you found *The FIRE Planner* helpful, please consider sharing it. You never know what ripple effect you may have on someone else.

Stay blessed.

# ACKNOWLEDGMENTS

Writing a book has always been on my FIRE bucket list. But somehow it always got pushed to the back of my priority list. When I finally made it a must, things started to fall into place and the right people showed up. I'd like to acknowledge some of these people here.

To start, I'd like to give a special thanks to Eszter Karpati for convincing me to take on this project, and for championing this book from concept to paper. The entire team at Quarto Publishing has been a dream to work with. Nikki Ellis and Gemma Wilson have laid out a beautiful book that makes FIRE approachable. Rachel Malig's copy editing skills are brilliant and intuitive. And many thanks to Kate Kirby and Samantha Warrington for green-lighting this special endeavor.

Thank you to Simon & Schuster for believing in this work and keeping us centered with valuable insights along the way.

Thank you to the entire FIRE community and these incredible FIRE leaders whose insight, inspiration, and contribution made this book much richer: Pete Adeney (Mr. Money Mustache), Carl Jensen (Mr. 1500), Brandon Ganch (Mad Fientist), Adam Fortuna (MinaFI), J. L. Collins (*Simple Path to Wealth*), and all of you who I featured or listed throughout. Without your drive to be more, do more, and give more, the FIRE movement wouldn't be possible.

To my high-level mastermind group Dustin Heiner, Tom Sylvester, and Adam Carroll, thank you guys for helping me to raise my standards to new levels. To Allan Fan and Marlon Smith, thank you for recognizing my voice and always encouraging me to play outside of my comfort zone.

And last but certainly not least, thank you to my family for supporting me throughout this entire process, being extra patient, and always believing in me.

For further information and resources on FIRE, go to www.financiallyalert.com /thefireplanner.

# GLOSSARY

**Assets** Things of value.

**Asset allocation** How your assets are distributed within different sectors or types of investments.

**BaristaFIRE** Has achieved financial independence (FI) and chooses to work part-time for supplemental income and/or access to benefits; a variation is if one spouse is retired and the other continues to work (by choice, not necessity).

**Bear market** Characterized as pulling back, negative, and shrinking. It's a term used to refer to a point when the market is 20% or lower than its previous value.

**Bull market** Characterized as positive, optimistic, and growing. It's a term used to refer to a point when the market is 20% or higher than its previous value.

**Cash flow (monthly)** Income minus expenses.

**Compound interest** Interest accrued on an initial balance that is also inclusive of accumulated interest from prior periods.

**Dollar cost averaging (DCA)** Strategy for investing in stocks over periodic intervals without worrying if the price of a stock is too high or too low.

**Entrepreneur** Someone who starts and/or undertakes the risk of a new business.

**Extreme Savings** Saving 70% or more of your household income.

**Fiduciary** Person or organization that acts in the best interest of their client.

**Financial independence (FI)** When passive income equals or exceeds your living expenses, and you're no longer reliant on earned income.

**FIRE** Abbreviation for "Financial Independence, Retire Early."

**FIRE number/Nest egg** 25 times your annual expenses; retirement principal from which you will withdraw your retirement.

**Geoarbitrage** Taking advantage of a lower cost of living in another geographic location without affecting quality of life.

**Hyperinflation** Inflation at a rapid rate leading to the devaluation of a currency.

**Income (active/earned)** Money that comes to you from active work (e.g., a job, a business you operate).

**Income (passive)** Money that you receive that doesn't require you to actively work (e.g., dividends, royalties, rental income, certain types of business income).

**Index fund** A mutual fund or ETF (exchange traded fund) that matches or tracks a particular stock market index.

**Inflation** The overall rise of prices and erosion of purchasing power.

**Intrapreneur** Employee who develops or champions an internal project or idea.

**Liabilities** Financial obligations (e.g., debt).

**Net worth** Assets minus liabilities.

**Passive stock market investing** Investing in the stock market with broad-based, low-cost index funds, and holding them for the long term.

**Recession** A period of economic contraction (typically a minimum of two quarters) in which gross domestic product declines and unemployment increases.

**Rehab** A real estate investing term used to describe the process of rehabilitating or restoring real property for profit.

**Real estate investing (REI)** The process of buying, selling, managing, renting, and/or engaging in related activities with real property for the purpose of profit.

**Stock market** An aggregate of exchanges (e.g., NYSE, NASDAQ, LSE, TSE) where shares of publicly listed companies are traded.

# NOTES

**Page 16:** https://www.bls.gov/news.release/cesan.nr0.htm.

**Page 16:** https://minafi.com/fire-meaning.

**Page 16:** https://www.physicianonfire.com/fatfire/.

**Page 20:** https://en.wikipedia.org/wiki/Personal_development.

**Page 23:** https://www.mrmoneymustache.com/2012/09/18/is-it-convenient-would-i-enjoy-it-wrong-question/.

**Page 26:** https://www.goodmorningamerica.com/living/story/couple-retired-early-40s-fire-method-58543615.

**Page 29:** https://www.investopedia.com/ask/answers/042415/what-average-annual-return-sp-500.asp.

**Page 29:** https://www.cnbc.com/2020/08/18/heres-a-list-of-stock-bull-markets-through-time-and-how-this-new-one-stacks-up.html.

**Page 29:** An index fund is a type of mutual fund or exchange-traded fund (ETF) with a portfolio constructed to match or track the components of a financial market index, such as Standard & Poor's 500 Index (S&P 500): https://www.investopedia.com/terms/i/indexfund.asp.

**Page 30:** https://www.cnn.com/2019/04/23/investing/bull-market-history/index.html.

**Page 64:** http://www.ascd.org/publications/educational-leadership/apr18/vol75/num07/The-Magic-of-Writing-Stuff-Down.aspx.

**Page 66:** https://www.investopedia.com/terms/f/four-percent-rule.asp.

**Page 66:** https://en.wikipedia.org/wiki/Trinity_study.

**Page 67:** chart based on https://www.campfirefinance.com/rule-of-25/.

**Page 80:** https://www.businessinsider.com/rich-famous-celebrities-who-lost-all-their-money-2018-5.

**Page 80:** https://www.tvovermind.com/20-celebrities-went-completely-broke/.

**Page 80:** https://www.chrishogan360.com/investing/how-much-of-your-income-to-invest-for-retirement.

**Page 82:** https://jamesclear.com/delayed-gratification.

**Page 84:** https://www.investopedia.com/terms/u/utility.asp.

**Page 85:** https://www.inc.com/logan-chierotti/harvard-professor-says-95-of-purchasing-decisions-are-subconscious.html.

**Page 89:** https://www.zumper.com/research/average-rent/los-angeles-ca?compare=tampa-fl.

**Page 92:** https://www.businessinsider.com/google-employee-lives-in-truck-in-parking-lot-2015-10#-3.

**Page 92:** https://www.forbes.com/sites/laurashin/2015/03/30/how-this-couple-retired-in-their-30s-to-travel-the-world/#5a9ae6de4dcf.

**Page 94:** https://en.wikipedia.org/wiki/FIRE_movement.

**Page 100:** https://about.vanguard.com/who-we-are/a-remarkable-history/Remembering_John_Bogle_transcript.pdf.

**Page 102:** https://jlcollinsnh.com/2014/06/10/stocks-part-xxiii-selecting-your-asset-allocation/.

**Page 116:** https://www.masterpassiveincome.com/single-family-home-rental.

**Page 120:** https://www.fundera.com/blog/small-business-employment-and-growth-statistics.

**Page 127:** https://engageme.online/google-innovation-employees/.

**Page 138:** https://www.jackcanfield.com/blog/how-to-create-an-empowering-vision-book/.

**Page 141:** https://www.cmu.edu/career/documents/my-career-path-activities/values-exercise.pdf.

**Page 148:** https://creativeplanning.com/blog/new-fiduciary-rule/.

**Page 168:** https://www.dictionary.com/browse/retirement.

**Page 172:** https://money.usnews.com/money/retirement/401ks/slideshows/9-ways-to-avoid-401-k-fees-and-penalties.

**Page 173:** https://www.investopedia.com/terms/r/rule72t.asp.

**Page 173:** the charts on pages 174 and 175 are based on https://www.madfientist.com/how-to-access-retirement-funds-early/.

**Page 174:** https://www.investopedia.com/terms/s/sequence-risk.asp.

**Page 183:** https://www.fitnesseducation.edu.au/blog/health/how-exercise-makes-you-happy/.

**Page 183:** https://www.helpguide.org/articles/healthy-eating/organic-foods.htm.

**Page 183:** https://www.healthline.com/nutrition/12-benefits-of-meditation.

**Page 185:** https://www.investopedia.com/articles/personal-finance/051315/will-vs-trust-difference-between-two.asp.

# INDEX

acceleration, income 86
achievable outcome 145,
160–61
achieving FIRE 22
action, taking 44, 155–56
active income 12, 56
additional income
worksheet 87
Adeney, Pete 23, 82
adjustments, making 158–59
aligned outcome 145
aligning actions 44
analysis paralysis 27
annual returns 29
art 186
asset allocation 48–49,
102–3
assets 48–49, 60

"Backdoor Roth IRA" 98
balance, finding 178
banknotes 51
BaristaFIRE 16, 26, 133, 180
bear markets 29, 174
beneficiaries, designated
185
bills 62
Bogle, John C. 100
bonus income 180
bucket list 166
"budgeted" numbers 64
bull markets 29, 30, 174
business liability 121

calculators, online 62
capital gains taxes 99
case studies 23–26, 90, 116,
126, 157
cash flow 56
cash flow properties 109,
112–13
characteristics, common
FIRE 15
coaching/teaching 186
compound interest 76–77,
161
consumerism 52–53, 80
contribution 21
COVID-19 30

CPI (consumer price index)
51
creativity, creating value
with 86, 88, 118–19
creativity beyond money
186
credit cards 53
credit score 48–49
currency 51

debt 48–49, 52–55, 92, 99,
117
DIKS (Dual Income Kids) 22
DINKS (Dual Income No
Kids) 22
dollar cost averaging (DCA)
29, 100
Dom (Gen Y Finance Guy)
25, 157
DOW Index 28

eating well 183
economic markets,
understanding 28–29
educate yourself 41
emergency fund 30
emotional purchases 85
emotions, cycle of investor
101, 102
empowering money beliefs
38, 44, 74–75
entrepreneurship 75, 96,
120–25
equation, FIRE 66–67
estate planning 185
evaluation 158
excess, cutting 83
exercise 183
exiting your job 176
expenses 48–49, 58–59, 68

Failsafe—Sequence of
Returns 174–75
family, future 68
FatFIRE 16–17, 68
Ferriss, Tim, *The 4-Hour
Work Week* 88
FI (Financial Independence)
12, 13, 68

FI Accelerators 56, 75, 96
"fiat currency" 51
fiduciary, fee-only 103,
148–49
financial snapshot 48–49
financing plans 52
FIRE movement 14–15
focusing on FI 74–75
food expenses 70, 89, 90,
183
4% Rule 66–67, 174
401k Retirement Plan 98,
176
FTSE 100 Index 28
fun, activities and 183

geoarbitrage 88–90
"get rich" schemes 96
gig economy 120
giving back 21
"gold standard" 51
Google 64, 127
GP (general partners) 114–15
grants 99
gratification 78, 82

habits, developing key
78–79
health care expenses 70, 89
healthy, living 183
Heiner, Dustin 24, 113, 116
home schooling 90
house hacking 26, 109,
110–11
housing expenses 70, 89,
90, 110
hustles, side 122–26
hyperinflation 51

income 12, 48–49, 86, 89
income acceleration 86
income sources 56–57, 93
index funds 100, 102–3
indexes, stock market
28–30
inflation 51
insurance, managing risk
with 132–33
insurance, types of 133, 185

intentional spending 84–85
interest, compound 76–77
internet, rise of 14
intrapreneurship 127–29
investing, extreme 75
investing in yourself 97
investing your time 97
investments 48, 62, 96–97
investor policy 103–6

Jensen, Carl 26, 111
journal, keeping a 41

LeanFIRE 16–17, 68
legacy, creating a wealth
    184
liabilities 48–49, 60
liability, business 121
limiting money beliefs 36,
    40–41
loans 52, 99

market cycles,
    understanding 28–29
measurable outcome 145
measuring results 45
meditation 183
metrics, key 48–49
metrics, tracking 62, 64–65
Microsoft Excel
    spreadsheets 64
milestones, map your
    152–54
mindset, money 34–43
monetary systems 51
money, movement of 51
money beliefs 34–43, 74–75
movement of money 51

NASDAQ Composite Index
    28
negotiation 130
net worth 60–61
number, FIRE (nest egg) 68,
    70–71
numbers, knowing your
    48–49, 64–65

outcomes 145, 147, 160–61

paid what you're worth,
    getting 130–31
pain, avoidance of 78

part-time work 169
passive income 12, 48, 56,
    66, 116
passive stock market
    investing 100–101
"paying yourself first" 80
personal expenses 70
personal growth 20
PI (passive investors) 114
positive people 41
post-FIRE 177–87
products, selling 121, 122
professional help 148–49
purchases, emotional 85

"raise laddering method"
    94–95
RE (Retire Early) 12, 13,
    168–71
real estate investing 75, 96,
    108–19
rebalancing 102–3
receipts 62
reflect and review 166–67
RegularFIRE 16–17
relocation 88–89
"representative money" 51
resourcefulness 30
results, measuring 45
ROI (return on investment)
    48
Roth IRA Conversion
    Ladder 90, 98, 172–73
Rule 72(t) 173
Rule of 25 66–68, 90
Rule of 72 77

S&P 500 Index 28–29
savings 62, 80–81, 86, 98
savings, extreme 75, 92–96
savings rate 48–49
scaling 121
Schroeder-Gardner, Michelle
    24, 126
seasonal work 181
self-directed IRA 99
self-sabotage, mitigating
    risks of 103
SEPP (Substantially Equal
    Periodic Payments) 173
service-based business 122
SIKS (Single Income Kids)
    22

SINKS (Single Income No
    Kids) 22
small businesses 99, 122
SMART goals 145–46
social contracts 78
software, financial 65
specific outcome 145, 147
spending, intentional 84–85
spending, retirement 68
spreadsheets, Excel/Google
    64
starting FIRE 27, 136
statements, financial 62
stock market 28–30, 100–101
strategy, FIRE 150–51
strengthening relationships
    worksheet 182
summary, FIRE plan 162
syndications, real estate
    109, 114–16

taxation 89, 98–99
technology, using 62–65
time, maximizing your 179
time tracking app 63
timed outcome 145
transportation expenses 70,
    89, 90
Travel Rewards 53
triple tax advantage 98
trust, revocable 185

unexpected, planning for
    the 30, 174
utilities expenses 89–90
"utility" 84

value, adding 127, 130
values exercise 141–44
Vanguard Group 100
variations, FIRE 16–17
vision board, FIRE 138–40,
    167
volunteering 182, 186

"why" pursue FIRE 18–19
wills 185
withdrawal strategies, early
    retirement 172–73
working, keep 169–70,
    180–81
writing 186